4/24

Heather & Michael,

Enjoy the Climb 🧗

Ed & Zoe Ann
Ps 46:10
1 Co 10:31

Also by Dr. Cerny

Learn to Market Yourself

Notes From the Coach

Old Coaches Never Die,
We Just Run Out of Time-outs!

An Adventure Through the 7 Levels of Change: Making a Difference Along the Way

By Dr. Ed Cerny

With Juliane & Rolf Smith

Coach's Corner Press
148 Citadel Dr.
Conway, SC 29526

Copyright © 2012 Ed Cerny

All Rights Reserved
Printed and bound in USA
First Printing 2012

For more information, please contact
The Coach's Corner Press
148 Citadel Dr.
Conway, SC 29526
843.347.5149   winners@sccoast.net
www.coached.com

Front Cover – The Matterhorn, Switzerland, Dr. Cerny
Back Cover – Paul Germeraad – Bohemian Hotel, Col. Rolf Smith (USAF ret.) on left Dr. Ed Cerny on the right
Back Cover Insert – Zach Cerny – Heart and Star Ranch, Fredericksburg, TX left to right Ed Cerny, Juliane Smith, Rolf Smith
Diagrams by Kelly Cerny Touchstone

Bible quotes from New International Version

ISBN 978-0-9661020-3-1

Printing provided by
Publishers Express Press
PO Box 99
Tony, WI 54563
1.800.255.9929

"Honor your father and your mother, so that you may live long in the land the LORD your God is giving you."

Exodus 20:12

These pages are dedicated to our parents:

Ed and Betsy Cerny
&
Art and Zoe Bushouse
&
Herbert and Irene Krause
&
Ralph and Sue Smith

Table of Contents

Preface		ix
Forward		xv
Introduction		xxi
Chapter 1	On the Trail of Becoming Drift-Free	1
Chapter 2	Having a Clear Focus	15
Chapter 3	Improving Little by Little	25
Chapter 4	What Can We Do Without	35
Chapter 5	Do What Others Have Done	45
Chapter 6	What's FAR OUT	53
Chapter 7	This is Impossible!	59
Chapter 8	God's Goals	69
About the Authors		91
Appreciation		97
Bibliography		99

Preface

HOW TO JOIN JESUS' TEAM
Pastor Bill Solomon, Montreat, NC

Bill Solomon is the man who led me to Christ on August 6, 1975 in Irmo, SC.

The context of this book is blatantly Christian. The author makes no apology for his Christian faith and its importance for you. Those in the coaching business know that the first step necessary for a young athlete to be on the team involves a joint decision to join with the team. No college student just sort of walks out of a physics class at 3:30 PM and just sort of walks onto the practice field and just sort of lines up at wide receiver and expects to be thrown the ball on a corner post pattern.

He must first contact the coaching staff and go through the process of being signed up as a team player after the coaches decide he is eligible and committed to their program. Just so, one cannot just waltz into God's program on Christian living and exclaim, *"Here I am, you lucky God. I'm going to make your team a winner by my great presence and ability!"* A private meeting with the Great Coach is a pre-requisite in order to get on His Team. Have you met with Jesus to get His perspective on life, what is important, His values, His plan, and His ultimate goal? In other words, have you changed from spectator status to player status on the inside of you? Have you committed your life to Jesus, the Savior? Are you really a Christian?

How does one become a Christian? Jesus made joining His team so simple that it borders on the unbelievable. There are 4 simple steps:

1) We must <u>CONFESS</u> that we are sinners and we need forgiveness for our sins. In many ways, we try to hide our

sins from others and from God. But, if the truth be known, we know down deep we are sinners and need forgiveness. Romans 3:23 states, *"For all have sinned and fall short of the glory of God."*

2) We must <u>TURN AWAY FROM</u> our sins. Turning away or "Repentance" means desire for a change in our thinking, our behavior and our values. We can't repent ourselves. But we can make the decision to allow God to turn our brain, our values and our behavior around from the wrong direction to the right direction. In His very first sermon on earth, in Mark 1:15, Jesus said to people *"Repent and believe the good news!"*

3) We must <u>BELIEVE THAT JESUS DIED ON THE CROSS</u> for our sins. We cannot accomplish this on our own. While living on earth around 2,000 years ago, Jesus was tried, sentenced, beaten, and killed on the cross for people's sins. He was punished for all the sins the human race had committed. He got up on the Cross and let us get down and go free. What a loving person Jesus was and is. He took away our sin and guilt by paying for it with His own death. Paul said it like this in 2 Corinthians 5:21, *"God made him who had no sin to be a sin offering for us, so that in Him we might become the righteousness of God."*

4) We need to ask Jesus for forgiveness through a <u>PRAYER OF COMMITMENT</u>, and invite Him to come into our life as our Savior and Lord. The following is a simple prayer to accomplish this:

"Dear Jesus, I am a sinner. I ask YOU for forgiveness of my sins. I want to turn my thinking and my actions in a new direction. I believe YOU died in my place for my sins. I invite YOU into my mind and my life. Change me to follow YOU as my personal Savior and Lord. Thanks for making me a Christian. In Your name I pray, Amen."

Upon praying this prayer, you became a member of His Team. You became a Christian.

Read on in this book for growth opportunities in this adventure and expedition of being a Christian.

GET READY FOR EXCITING, STUPENDOUS, AND WONDERFUL LIFE CHANGES!

Climbing the Mountain with Jesus
Pastor Ronny Byrd, Palmetto Shores Church, Myrtle Beach, SC

Ronny Byrd has been my pastor since 1992.

Over the past fifteen years, I have completed twelve marathons. Eleven of my runs have been near my house in Myrtle Beach. In fact, the course passes in both directions exactly one block from each side of my house. This past year, because of some medical treatments, I chose not to register for the marathon. However, on the morning of the race I could not stand it.

At 7:30 I put on my running gear and started running from my street at the fourteen mile marker toward the starting line. Within a mile, a few of the lead runners passed me. I continued for about another mile, then turned around and started running with the pack. It was awesome! I had never been with a group like that at mile fourteen. The feeling was incredible. Then reality hit. I remembered I was not in the race.

I was dressed like the other runners. I looked just like the other runners. I smelled just like the other runners. But something very important was different about me. I had not registered for the race. Imagine me trying to enter the finish chute at the end of the race where an announcer calls out the name of the finishers and having a course manager pulling me from the pack because I had NO number or registration credentials. The feeling was incredible until I realized the fact – I was not even in the race.

In Luke 18, Jesus shares a story about a young man who discovered this dilemma with something far more important than a sporting event. In essence, Jesus gave this man the same news. In order to participate in eternal life, one must properly join the team (climb the mountain, run the race). Take a look at this story, and then make sure you have established your personal relationship with Jesus and properly "registered for the race."

The Rich Man and the Kingdom of God

Luke 18:18-23

[18] *A certain ruler asked him, "Good teacher, what must I do to inherit eternal life?"*

[19] *"Why do you call me good?" Jesus answered. "No one is good—except God alone.* [20] *You know the commandments: 'You shall not commit adultery, you shall not murder, you shall not steal, you shall not give false testimony, honor your father and mother.'"*

[21] *"All these I have kept since I was a boy," he said.*

[22] *When Jesus heard this, he said to him, "You still lack one thing. Sell everything you have and give to the poor, and you will have treasure in heaven. Then come, follow me."*

[23] *When he heard this, he became very sad, because he was very wealthy.*

Every parable Jesus told had a main point and this point usually offended some people. It may appear that Jesus was picking on rich people, but that was certainly not the point. When he said, "You still lack one thing," he was referring to ANYTHING anyone chooses to put ahead of one hundred percent allegiance to knowing and following God's perfect plan. And that plan begins, continues and ends with making Jesus the authority of every area of life. So, it is critically important to make sure you join Jesus' team according to his plan. Keep reading and make sure you have appropriately registered to join his team!

Forward

Rolf Smith shares how he came to write <u>The 7 Levels of Change</u>. This will help you understand the connection between his book and <u>An Adventure Through the 7 Levels of Change</u>.

The Evolution of the 7 Levels of Change

While working in Exxon's Innovations Group in Marketing I was asked to figure out how to connect Quality's "continuous improvement" and innovation. Being a mathematician by background, I began by looking for common denominators. It struck me that they were both all about ideas. Creativity is about having ideas and innovation and continuous improvement are about implementing idea. Both start with an idea. Both depend on coming up with ideas and that requires creativity. Both lead to changes when the ideas are implemented and my common denominators were:

- Ideas
- Creativity
- Change
- Implementation

Bingo! creativity & ideas => change & implementation => Continuous Improvement. The overall common denominators running through all that were the letters "C" and "I". And if I added Continuous Innovation it led to a simple equation:

- $CI = ci = ci = CI$

That flashed me back to the Air Force Chief of Staff's Innovation Task Force that I had been part of - and the first military Office of Innovation launched as a result. We had come up with a simple formula for Innovation:

IDEA
+
CREATIVITY
+
ENHANCEMENT
+
EVALUATION
+
IMPLEMENTATION

INNOVATION!

And there were ideas, creativity, implementation and innovation again – **CI**

I had an insight: People tend to generalize "change" – however, not all change is the same. There are little changes and very big changes – "orders" of change:

1st Order Change: Smaller or incremental change that occurs within a given system which remains unchanged. "Continuous improvement" seemed to fit here.

2nd Order Change: Larger change whose scope and occurrence changes the system itself. This seemed to fit with what most people described as "innovation".

To the best of my recollection, that's when I first began experimenting with the idea of levels of change and came up with three Levels:

1. **Continuous Improvement**: Doing the right things and doing things right
2. **Adaptation:** Copying things other organizations are doing
3. **Different:** Doing things that no one is doing or that haven't been done.

Adapting the work of quality gurus W. Edwards Deming and William Conway, and working with some of the best minds in management – my corporate clients – these gradually evolved from three initial levels into a model with five levels:

1. **Efficiency:** Doing things right
2. **Effectiveness:** Doing the right things
3. **Cutting:** Stopping doing things. Eliminating waste.
4. **Copying:** Benchmarking - Doing things others are doing
5. **Different:** Doing things that no one is doing or that haven't been done

Based on the order in which these "Levels" seemed to naturally progress, I switched Levels 1 and 2 and added "Improving" as Level 3 - which built on the first two Levels. This took the model to six levels with Level 6 becoming "Innovation" – a new and different 2nd Order result that had the potential to change the entire system that it was part of:

1. **Effectiveness:** Doing the right things
2. **Efficiency:** Doing the right things right
3. **Improving:** Doing the right things better
4. **Cutting:** Stopping doing things. Eliminating waste.
5. **Copying:** Benchmarking - Doing things others are doing
6. **Different:** Doing things that haven't been done

Adding "Impossible" – doing something that can't be done was a big leap. Everyone to whom I tried to explain it gave me a great deal of pushback on the concept. How could you do something that couldn't be done? And this is when I began formally using "Levels" with the model. And "Different" became "Diff*f*erent" (for really different!):

Level 1: Effectiveness - Doing the right things
Level 2: Efficiency - Doing the right things right
Level 3: Improving - Doing the right things better
Level 4: Cutting - Stopping doing things. Eliminating waste.
Level 5: Copying - Benchmarking - Doing things others are doing
Level 6: Diff*f***erent** - Doing things that haven't been done
Level 7: Breakthrough - Doing things that can't be done – the Impossible

The number "7" was not a deliberate choice but rather one I arrived at empirically over time. I also saw pretty clearly that Levels 1-5 were the basics of Continuous Improvement and that Levels 5-7 were the basis for Continuous Innovation.

The 7 Levels evolved into their sequence because the sequence works, yet the concepts aren't increasingly difficult as they progress through the levels. They build on each other as they go – oootching upwards. The changes they deal with, however, are typically more difficult to sell and to implement as they climb toward Level 7. Yet, you don't have to go through all of the lower levels of change to make a Level 6 or 7 Change.

Every School for Innovators has been an operational research and development cauldron for the 7 Levels of Change. Sparked by the insights we were gaining by using the 7 Levels of Change coupled with rock-climbing and low level mountaineering in the School for Innovators, I hit on the idea of "Thinking Expeditions" to operationalize the 7 Levels and leverage the ongoing stream of discoveries, learnings, tools and techniques coming out of the School. The School for innovators had become our R&D center.

We began to use the mountaineering metaphor as the baseline design for operational Thinking Expeditions built around a wide variety of major challenges facing some of the world's largest corporations – Exxon, British Petroleum, Procter & Gamble, EDS, General Mills, Johnson & Johnson, and the U.S Navy's SMART SHIP – and led teams to achieve startling and exciting breakthrough results over the whole range of the 7 Levels of Change.

Once we had embedded the Thinking Expedition process model as the backbone of the Schools, we began to discover a variety of ways to apply the concept of the 7 Levels as a creative problem solving tool - and to develop supporting processes and techniques for the model in large organizations.

Since 1997, when the 7 Levels of Change was first published, we have run forty-nine Schools for Innovators. As soon as the book was published I began using it as a Field guide for both the School and for Thinking Expeditions. For the last several years it has also been adopted the textbook for Disney University's Creativity & Innovation college class.

Change can be very difficult for companies of any size as well as for individuals. By breaking down change into different levels for my clients, I found them surprisingly successful at making significant changes that affected not only the company's bottom line but also its future path of success.

In the School for Innovators, I found our graduates making profound changes in their lives. When we integrated the structure of the 7 Levels of Change and the 7 Levels of Thinking into Me, Inc. (the process we developed to help our graduates set new strategic directions and mentally incorporate themselves), they exploded with energy, commitment, and self confidence.

And now the 7 Levels of Change are evolving further, moving into new Levels of Exploration and Thinking with Ed

Cerny's Pro-Vision™ of using them as the framework for an exciting spiritual Journey.

May God bless your Adventures Through the 7 Levels of Change.

Rolf C. Smith, Jr.
Colonel, USAF (ret)
Fredericksburg, Texas
March 2012

Introduction

How This Book Came to be Written

I read Rolf's book for the first time in 2000. It was an eye opening experience, but I felt the book was over my head and I really wasn't prepared to deal with the 7 Levels of Change and what differences they would make in my life.

Over the next 11 years I talked about the book in my business classes, but I never ventured beyond talking about the concepts. In 2011 I contacted Rolf to see if I might be able to participate in one of his Adventures in Thinking Diff*f*erently at his School for Innovators.

Rolf was kind enough to invite me to participate as an "outside stretcher." So, October 28th through November 1st, 2011, I joined Rolf and ten others who were veterans of Rolf's creative expeditions at the Bohemian Hotel in Celebration, FL.

It was a life-changing expedition. My purpose was to see if it was possible to help a person grow through using of the 7 Levels of Change from a Christian perspective. The following section is taken directly from Rolf's book, with his permission.

"The 7 Levels of Change go from easy to impossible - across a spectrum of continual change (*continuous innovation*) through increasing levels of difficulty. Each level is progressively more complex, more different, more challenging to undertake that the preceding level."

After meeting Rolf, I realized that he lives the 7 Levels of Change. He drops them into conversations. He uses them in his everyday life. He writes about them. The levels of change model can be superimposed on your personal vision and then imbedded within your goals, life, and day-to-day operating environment - into the way you think. That is why when Rolf created the "THIИK Expedition" he had the T typed upside down and the N typed backwards, so we would think differently!

I needed an easy way to remember the 7 Levels of Change, too. The Lord gave me a way to do just that. He gave me **BƎ LIƎ FS!®** The backward "Ǝ" in **BƎ LIƎ FS!®** is there to remind me, as Col. Smith says, "To Get Diff*f*erent Results one must Think Diff*f*erent!" (not "differently")

How many times did you count the letter "f" in Diff*f*erent? It's not a typo; Col. Smith deliberately added a third "*f*" in italics to the word. It's catchy in a subtle way, isn't it?

What follows is a book about change and growth as a Christian. The first seven chapters are constructed to follow the 7 Levels of Change. We are going on an adventure that leads to an expedition in climbing a virtual mountain, the Mountain of **BƎ LIƎ FS!®**. We will be roped together as part of a mountain climbing team. In order to safely ascend, summit and safely descend, we have to work as a team to accomplish our objective.

Rolf has asked me to be our team's lead guide and Juliane, Rolf's wife, will be climbing with us to keep us straight on the climb as editor-in-guide and base camp manager. Rolf has requested to be the outside stretcher on the team with the 7 Levels of Change. We have prayerfully asked Jesus Christ to be our high altitude guide.

Dr. John Tolson is a friend of mine. He is the former Dallas Cowboy Chaplain. Recently he published a new book written for men, <u>Take a Knee: Winning Plays for the Game of Life</u>. It is a 31 day thought provoking devotional book. Day 30 opens up with Proverbs 27:17, *"As iron sharpens iron, so one man sharpens another."*

Dr. Tolson goes on to explain, "I'm convinced every man needs a mentor to help keep his head screwed on straight and a handful of peers to offer the occasional swift kick in the rear. I've seen lots of athletic careers in my service to professional teams. The guys who made it far, never got there alone."

We don't want to climb our Mountain of **BƎ LIƎ FS!®** alone either. That's why we will always climb as a team.

Growing up I remember attending several Boy Scout camps. We always had to have a swim buddy to get near the water. It's the same way on the mountain. To be safe, we need to climb together.

I took the photograph of the Matterhorn on the front of our book back in 2008 when my wife, Zoe Ann, and I were on a trip in Germany and Switzerland. My youngest daughter, Kelly, created the graphics to explain the 7 Levels of Change in light of climbing this virtual mountain, the Mountain of **BƎ LIƎ FS!®**.

So now, The Mountain of B∃ LI∃ FS!® is easier for me to remember and apply.

Level 1 is **B**e Effective – more in Chapter 1 at Camp 1

Level 2 is be ∃fficient – more in Chapter 2 at Camp 2

Level 3 is **L**ittle by **L**ittle – more in Chapter 3

Level 4 is **I**nclude/Exclude – more in Chapter 4

Level 5 is ∃xample – more in Chapter 5

Level 6 is **F**ar Out – more in Chapter 6

Level 7 is **S**eems Impossible – more in Chapter 7

Ed Cerny
Conway, SC
March, 2012

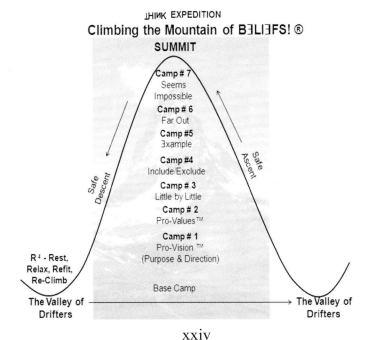

Chapter 1

On the Trail of Becoming Drift-Free

"The Fear of the Lord is the beginning of knowledge, but fools despise wisdom and instruction." Proverbs 1:7

B – Be Effective
1st Level of Change
Camp 1
The Parable of the Talents paraphrased from Matthew 25-14-30

A man was leaving on a journey. He gave bags of gold to three of his servants. He gave one servant five bags, to another he gave two bags and to a third, he gave one bag.

While the master was away on his journey, the first servant was able to double the five bags of gold to ten bags. The second servant was able to increase his two bags of gold to four bags. But the third servant took his only bag of gold and buried it in the ground.

Upon the master's return, he asked each servant to show what he had done with the bags of gold. The master was most pleased with the work of the first two servants. But he was most displeased with the lazy servant who returned only the one bag he was given because the servant was afraid to take any risks.

A real life example of this parable might be as follows. I recently had a dream about this parable. I had received a check for one million dollars. What I thought about day and night was, **"What does the Lord want me to do with the money?"**

I was so focused on what to do and not wanting to make a mistake that I forgot that I had never made out a will. And I forgot to endorse the check, as well.

I never put the money in the bank! I was focused on the wrong thing – I was afraid of making a mistake.

The next week in my dream I died, and since I had not done anything with the check, no one was able to receive the benefits from the check. I had not used my talent wisely.

That's a very sad dream. I believe it also saddens God's heart, too. He has given each of us certain talents to be used to further His kingdom on earth. Sadly, many of us never use those talents – just like the third servant in the parable. The same is true of the dream I had in which I had never cashed the check.

My question to myself is, "What can I do to use the God-given talents I have been given?" Author Napoleon Hill (1883-1970) states in his book, Outwitting the Devil (2011), "Ninety-eight percent of the people in the world are drifting through life with no plan or purpose. This is the major cause of failure."

The Devil has a whole host of tools he uses against us. He utilizes tools like fear, procrastination, and poverty to keep us in line. These are his main weapons causing us to daily drift through life.

If that is true, how can we become Drift-Free? How can we become two per-centers (98% + 2% = 100%)? Two per-centers are those people who live on the earth and are focused and have a clear sense of purpose and direction!

Everyone on the earth, over 7 billion of us, live in the Valley of Drifters. In fact, that's where each of us was born – in the Valley of Drifters. Unless we deliberately do something to rise above the valley, we will be there forever. Because we are born sinners, we <u>all</u> start out in the Valley of Drifters.

Climbing the Mountain of B∃ LI∃ FS!®

We are going to make an attempt to safely climb the Mountain of **B∃ LI∃ FS!**® and safely return. It won't be an easy climb. There will be lots of obstacles and challenges on the mountain.

Our Base Camp is just above the Valley of Drifters. This is where we will start our adventure and later our expedition. We will have to carefully plan how we're going to attack the mountain. What are the supplies we'll need to successfully ascend and safely descend? And we'll need to store all our supplies in a secure area.

Where will we obtain the funds necessary to purchase our supplies? Where will we obtain the talents necessary to make a successful round trip from the Valley of Drifters to the summit of the mountain and a safe return back down to the Valley of Drifters? Our Lord will supply.

Just above the Base Camp is Camp 1 – The "**B**e Effective" Camp. If you are confused, look at the mountain drawing at the end of this chapter.

Life Verse

We need to prepare ourselves to leave the base camp and be ready to climb on up to Camp 1. How will we do that?

As a Christian, one of the best ways I know to prepare for all the adversity life throws at us is to have a sense of purpose and a positive sense of direction. One of the very best ways I know to accomplish this goal is to have a life verse.

Having a life verse to call on is essential whenever you come to an area in your life that requires wisdom or to get out of a rut or to help you combat the devil.

We are all made up of flesh and blood. But as a Christian, we are different in that we can call upon the Holy Spirit to provide us with wisdom in all circumstances, and our personal life verse can remind us of this.

As Christians, we will face obstacles or challenges in our lives every day. To me, obstacles are negative. Challenges, on the other hand, appear to be positive in nature. The difference is our attitude and approach to the challenges in our lives.

We can start facing a challenge by remembering our life verse first, before we do anything else. It gives us a way to look at a situation in a positive light, a different light, a Spiritual light.

Now, if you don't have a life verse, don't fret. As you climb the mountain, it will come to you. You'll see.

I didn't have a life verse when I first became a Christian. In fact, I drifted in my life for most of the first two years after I professed belief in Jesus Christ!

It wasn't until later that my life verse was revealed to me while I was sitting in church. Pastor Solomon, the man who led me to Christ in 1975, was also the person who spoke the words that shaped my life verse.

My life verse comes from 1 Corinthians 10:31, *"Whatever you do, whether you eat or drink or whatever you do, do it all to the glory of God."* The Lord has given me a method to make it easy to remember scripture.

Since in the middle of a challenge it is hard to remember all those words, the Lord gave me a term some time ago that I use daily to stay focused on what is important in my life. The term is Pro-Vision™. A Pro-Vision™ is made up of only three to six words of the verse that gives you a sense of purpose and positive direction.

My personal Pro-Vision™ based on my life verse from 1 Corinthians 10:31 is "To Glorify God." I ask myself when I am faced with a challenge, "How can I glorify God with my response to this challenge?"

Reaction vs. Response

What is the difference between a reaction and a response to an obstacle or a challenge? To me, a reaction is being only human. It's what we naturally do. Oftentimes, that can get us into trouble. On the other hand, responding to a challenge is positive. The choice is ours to make.

Do I always make the right response? No, I am not God. I do try to reflect before I respond, and there are times that I realize afterwards that I could have handled the situation differently.

My goal is to sin less today than I did yesterday. Will I ever become 100% sinless? No. But that doesn't excuse me from not trying.

Dr. Paul Stoltz is a mountain climber by choice. He does it for fun. He is also the author of Adversity Quotient: Turning Obstacles into Opportunities and Adversity Quotient @ Work: Making Everyday Challenges the Key to Your Success. Additionally, Dr. Stoltz has written another book with Erik Weihenmayer (the first blind person to ever climb the 7 tallest peaks on the 7 continents) The Adversity Advantage: Turning Everyday Struggles into Everyday Greatness. Paul says, **"Purpose defines your mountain and how far you move forward and up along the slopes; it is the extent to which you will ultimately succeed."**

Mountain of B3 LI3 FS!®

In climbing the Mountain of **B3 LI3 FS!®, w**e are facing a big challenge. Will we successfully make the ascent and the subsequent descent as a team or not? Do we have a big enough purpose to sustain us with all the adversity we'll face along the way?

The first letter in the Mountain of **B3 LI3 FS!®** is "**B**". It stands for "**B**e Effective." The best way I know how to be effective in my life is to live out my personal Pro-Vision™ every day. This is the essence of Camp 1. Without an Effective Pro-Vision™, we can't climb any higher. Or at the very least, without having a Pro-Vision™, we won't be as effective as we could be in our climb.

My Pro-Vision™ has to be such an integral part of my life that I should be able to call on it in a split second. I should not have to think about it. It is my first line of defense in all that I do and say. That's why it needs to be short and to the point.

Another way to look at a situation is to ask yourself, "Would I want what I am about to say or do in the next 10 seconds to be broadcast around the world on You-Tube®?" If the answer is "No," or "I'm not sure," then don't do it! It's pretty simple to remember when we have a Pro-Vision™ to respond to, isn't it?

Coach John Wooden

Let's look at another example of a Pro-Vision™ from my long distance mentor. His name is Coach John Wooden. Coach Wooden died in 2010 – just short of his 100th birthday. He was the UCLA men's basketball coach from 1948 to 1975.

He still inspires me. Early on in my high school coaching career, I came across the first book that he ever wrote, <u>They Call Me Coach</u>.

In the book, Coach Wooden explained his coaching philosophy, "Success is peace of mind which is a direct result of self-satisfaction in knowing you did your best to become the best that you are capable of becoming." In all of Coach Wooden's years of coaching, he never asked any of his players or teams to win a single game. He only asked each player to do his best.

He inspired me long before I ever thought of having a Pro-Vision™. He was responsible for me changing my coaching philosophy from trying to win at all costs to helping players and people to "Do their best."

I corresponded with Coach Wooden from the early 1980s until deep into the 21st Century. I only met the man once, but that was enough to make a life changing difference in my life.

In 1988 I was the president of our local advertising club while I was a marketing professor at the then University of South Carolina – Coastal campus in Conway, SC.

That year the American Advertising Federation's National Convention was held in Los Angles, California. Some twenty years earlier I had lived with my parents and brothers in Southern California, so I was familiar with the location of the convention.

I had a family of my own and I wanted to take them out west to explore some of the places in Southern California before the convention began. I also wrote Coach Wooden to see if we could visit with him. He invited us to his townhouse in Encino, California.

Coach Wooden treated us like we were part of his family. We spent the whole afternoon with him.

We took some photographs to commemorate the moment.

And I've included one of the notes Coach Wooden sent me. The next page includes the Cerny family in June 1988 at Coach Wooden's home.

The Cernys at Coach Wooden's home
L to R: Ed, Coach Wooden, Jenny, Zach & Carrie

L to R: Kelly, Zoe Ann, Coach Wooden, Jenny, Zach & Carrie

L to R: Sheepie, Coach Wooden, Kelly & Zach

From the desk of...
JOHN WOODEN

3-21-86

Dear Ed,

Your words of commendation were very kind and deeply appreciated as is your interest. Many thanks for taking the time to express yourself.

It always pleases me to learn that my "Pyramid" has been meaningful to others.

Sometimes I think I may be much like the one who said, "I am not what I ought to be, not what I want to be, not what I am going to be, but I am thankful that I am not what I used to be." I am certain that the development of and trying to live up to the philosophy presented has made me a better person than I would have been, even though I fall short of what I should be and would like to be.

Through the years three different ministers have sent me their ideas of what scriptures fit in to the blocks of the pyramid and some coincided with yours.

It was one year ago today that I lost my dear Nellie and I am having trouble continuing this. Please understand and pray for me.

Sincerely,
John Wooden

I really appreciated Coach Wooden writing me to pray for him. I prayed for him and his family until the day he died. And I still continue to pray for his growing family.

Over the past thirty years I have read "Our Daily Bread" every day. Allow me to close this section on Coach Wooden with one of "Our Daily Bread" readings. It addresses the issue of team work.

The Wooden Rule
October 16, 2011— *by <u>Cindy Hess Kasper</u>*

Legendary UCLA basketball coach John Wooden had an interesting rule for his teams. Whenever a player scored, he was to acknowledge the person on the team who had assisted. When he was coaching high school, one of his players asked, "Coach, won't that take up too much time?" Wooden replied, "I'm not asking you to run over there and give him a big hug. A nod will do."

To achieve victory on the basketball court, Wooden saw the importance of teaching his players that they were a team—not "just a bunch of independent operators." Each person contributed to the success of everyone else.

That reminds me of the way the body of Christ should work. According to 1 Corinthians 12:19-20, each of us is a separate part of one body. "If they were all one member, where would the body be? But . . . there are many members, yet one body." Is the success of a pastor, a Bible study, or a church program based solely on one person's accomplishments? How many people contribute to the smooth operation of a church, a Christian organization, a family?

Coach Wooden's rule and 1 Corinthians 12 are both rooted in the principle of seeing our need for one another. Let's use our gifts within the body of Christ to build up, strengthen, and help to carry out God's purposes (vv.1-11).

The Coach's Corner

In 1995 I created an Encouragement Business entitled, The Coach's Corner®. I have a Pro-Vision™ for the business, too. "Building Leaders, Achieving Goals." It helps me stay focused on exactly what I do – no more, no less. I am an "Encouragement Coach."

Now, it's your turn to get into the game I want to encourage you to create your own Pro-Vision™ from your own life verse.

Next, listen to how the Lord is leading you to create your own personal Pro-Vision™ from your life verse. Remember: a Pro-Vision™ is "Three to six words that gives you a sense of purpose and positive direction."

Write your own personal Pro-Vision™ here:

How does that make you feel?

What difference will it make in your life from today onward?

Is it difficult for you to answer these questions? Keep trying.

You are on your way to becoming a Drift-Free person! You are on your way now to becoming one of the few two per-center people in the world.

To recall what we've done at Camp 1, the goal is to **Be** Effective. This is the Level 1 of Change. We have accomplished this by creating a Pro-Vision™. This will give us a sense of purpose and positive direction in our lives.

Now let's climb higher up the Mountain of **BƎ LIƎ FS!**®. Let's hike up to Camp 2.

Behind every Level of Change there is a corresponding **Level of Fear**. Fear is driven by reversed thinking - what could go wrong as opposed to what could go right. The Levels of Fear surface rapidly during a Thinking Expedition as we move as a team through the 7 Levels of Change and their corresponding 7 Levels of Thinking.

Level 1 Level of Fear: Paralysis

Level 1 is the Level of Fear of Paralysis. It is the Fear of doing the wrong things. So, we do nothing!

We overcome this level of fear by doing something. The old Nike slogan comes to mind, "Just Do It!"

THINK EXPEDITION
Climbing the Mountain of BELIEFS! ®

- **SUMMIT**
- **Camp # 7** — Seems Impossible
- **Camp # 6** — Far Out
- **Camp #5** — Example
- **Camp #4** — Include/Exclude
- **Camp # 3** — Little by Little
- **Camp # 2** — Pro-Values™
- **Camp # 1** — Pro-Vision™ (Purpose & Direction)
- **Base Camp**

Safe Descent / Safe Ascent

R^4 - Rest, Relax, Refit, Re-Climb

The Valley of Drifters → The Valley of Drifters

Now, let's climb to Camp 2.

Chapter 2

Having a Clear Focus

"I will instruct you and teach you in the way you should go; I will counsel you with my loving eye on you." Psalm 32:8

Ǝ – Ǝfficient
2nd Level of Change
Camp 2

The backward "Ǝ" **in Ǝfficient** reminds me to continue to think differently as we continue to climb the Mountain of **BƎ LIƎ FS!®**

The Feeding of the 5000 paraphrased from John 6:1-15

Jesus was speaking to a crowd of over 5000 men in a remote region. The people appeared hungry, and Jesus wanted to test his disciples to see how they would respond.

Jesus wanted to know where they would get enough bread to feed such a large crowd. They didn't know, but one disciple said that a boy had brought five small loaves of bread and two small fish.

Jesus asked the crowd to sit in the grass. He blessed the food, and the disciples began passing out the bread and fish. Jesus then asked the disciples to gather up what was left over after everyone had eaten. They collected twelve baskets full of bread!

There are several interesting points about this Scripture reading.

<u>First</u> Jesus performed this miracle because the disciples did not know what to do – they wanted to send the crowd away to purchase food on their own. Our Lord knew

better. He blessed the small amount of food provided, and it was enough to satisfy everyone with twelve baskets of food left over – one basket for each of the disciples to fill – a great lesson for the disciples!

Point Number 2 Someone had to have the foresight to bring food to the gathering in the first place. That means that the boy had to plan in advance to purchase the bread or someone else had to bake it beforehand. Someone had to catch the fish and remember to bring them along, too.

Point Number 3 The boy who brought the food did not hoard the food and had not eaten it beforehand. The boy was disciplined enough to wait to eat the food he had brought.

Point Number 4 The boy brought only enough for himself not others. If he had prepared to bring the food but in his haste to see Jesus had not brought the food along, then there would have been nothing to bless.

Point Number 5 The boy gave the food to the disciples to give to Jesus. He was not selfish, but rather he was selfless.

These five points bring clarity to the concept of being efficient. In the previous chapter we discussed what it takes to be effective. It takes having a Pro-Vision™ - one that can be used instantly

How Do We Become Efficient?

For every situation, we need to take some time to think through what our non-negotiable values are. Many people have never thought of what their own personal values are. They just go through life moving from one thing or situation or one person to another, aimlessly drifting.

Before we travel higher up the mountain, we need to take some time by ourselves, without any distractions, and think through what our values actually are. Try to list between five and seven values. This process might take some time, so don't be discouraged as you climb the mountain. My non-negotiable values are:

Pro-Values™

Our Lord also gave me the term Pro-Values™. These values need to match up with our Pro-Vision™. Let me give you an example to show you how it works.

My Pro-Vision™ for my company, The Coach's Corner® is "Building Leaders, Achieving Goals." My personal Pro-Vision™ is "To Glorify God."

My set of Pro-Values™ for both Pro-Visions™ is wrapped around the acrostic

C-O-A-C-H

This is what is on the back of my business card:

C - Christ Centered

The first "C" stands for "Christ Centered." I strive every day to keep Christ in the center of my life, not an afterthought that I use only when I am in trouble.

O - Opportunity to Grow

The "O" stands for "Opportunity to Grow." The only way we can grow is to take calculated risks to get better or be better than we were yesterday.

A - All-Star (Shine Brightly Each Day)

The "A" stands for "All-Star – to shine brightly each day." I have a choice each day in terms of my attitude. One, I can greet each day in a negative manner or two, I can greet each day in a positive manner. The choice is entirely mine. Don't allow circumstances to dictate your attitude – you choose your attitude first.

C - Congratulate (Help Others Smile)

The second "C" stands for "Congratulate – help others smile." I believe you can help others smile by acknowledging in a positive way that you appreciate the little things people do. Compliment others on how they answer the phone or go out of their way to do something for someone else.

H - Healthy – Run Your Game Plan

And finally, the "H" stands for "Healthy – run your game plan." Living a healthy lifestyle is a deliberate form of discipline. Just like the boy in the parable who came to hear Jesus speak, he was the only one who brought anything along to eat! He was a two per-center!

You cannot decide to eat healthy if you don't plan ahead. You have to shop for the healthy foods first. It doesn't do any good to say you're going to eat healthy, but you never start. You never put a plan into action.

It is the same way with exercising for health. I have been working out on a regular basis in some form since 1960 - since I was thirteen years old.

I was tired of being beaten up all the time – I was a very skinny boy growing up. I got permission from my parents

to become a newspaper boy and delivered the r
on my bicycle.

The first money I made, I got my dad to drive me to local Sears store, and I purchased a 110 pound set of weights. No one in my neighborhood was lifting weights, so I taught myself how to lift.

Since then it has become one of the great joys of my life — working out. I love to work out. Over the years, my lifting style has changed to accommodate my stage in life. After I do my early morning Bible study and take my dog for a walk, I head to the gym.

Let me give you another example of having a set of Pro-Values™. In the previous chapter, I spoke about my long distance mentor, Coach John Wooden. In 1922, when Coach Wooden was twelve years old, his father gave John a 7 point creed by which to live.

He wanted his son to:

Be true to yourself

Make each day your masterpiece

Help others

Drink deeply from good books

Make friendship a fine art

Build a shelter against a rainy day

Pray for guidance & give thanks for your blessings every day.

thor Pat Williams has written an insightful book on this subject entitled, <u>Coach Wooden: The 7 Principles That Shaped His Life and Will Change Yours</u>. It might give you some new ways to examine your own Pro-Values™.

What are your values? What values are non-negotiable?

I have heard it said, if you want to know what kind of values a person has, look at the kind of friends a person associates with on a daily basis. That might be a good indication of a person's values. What might people say about your values knowing the kinds of folks you hang out with?

I have also heard it said if you are the smartest person in your group, you need to find another group! You'll never grow being the smartest person in the room. Expand your horizons.

From another perspective I have heard you can tell people's values by how they spend their time each day. If someone followed you around all day, what would your values say about you? Are you pleased with what people might discover about you?

I have also heard that you can understand people's values by the things they spend their money on! Think that might be true? If someone was able to look at your bank and credit card statements, what might that say about you? Would you be pleased to show someone your statements?

Let me give you a third example of how important a Pro-Vision™ and set of Pro-Values™ might be. In 1995 I was invited to help a family-owned business in Myrtle Beach, SC, become more focused.

Ocean Lakes Family Campground created its own Pro-Vision™ of "We create family memories that last a lifetime." Go to their website, and you'll find that the Pro-Vision™ has stayed the same all these years.

www.oceanlakesfamilycampground.com

Since the company already had a big starfish mascot, the company created a set of Pro-Values™ around the 8 letters of STARFISH.

The story doesn't end there. When I first started working with the leadership team, I asked them if there was a national campground association.

They said "yes," but in order to win an award your campground needed to be located in California. They explained that only California camp sites ever won the National Campground of the Year Award.

But, nevertheless, I continued to ask them to apply. For months they did not apply.

Finally, in 1996 they applied…and lost! But the leadership of Ocean Lakes learned what they needed to do in order to improve. They went to work on making the improvements.

With the changes came their first National Campground of the Year Award in 1997!

And they won again in 1999...

and again in 2002...

and again in 2008...

and most recently in 2011!

They have won the award of National Campground of the Year five times now. But they never would have won if they had never tried and if they had not overcome their first failure.

Remember, my Pro-Vision™ for the Coach's Corner® is "Building Leaders, Achieving Goals." And one of my Pro-Values™ is to help others have an "Opportunity to Grow." It is pure joy to watch others succeed.

It is important to know what your values are in life so that you can stick with them through any adversity and/or challenge you face. They need to become part of your daily life.

Strive to create an acrostic that will remind you what your non-negotiable values are.

Create a set of Pro-Values™ based upon your own non-negotiable values.

The values should match up with your Pro-Vision™.

Write your set of Pro-Values™ here:

Are you pleased with the results? Would you be pleased to show them to others? Would you be pleased to have them printed on the back of your business cards?

Level 2 Level of Fear: Inefficiency

Level 2 is the Level of Fear of Inefficiency. It is the fear of wasting time. It is the fear of doing the right things wrong. To fight this tendency on the climb, tie into your team and solve challenges together.

Mountain climbing is best done with others, rather than by yourself. We need each other. We rejoice and suffer together. It's safer and more enjoyable. It's good to be the encourager for each other.

Juliane Smith after reading the manuscript for the first time was able to come up with her own Pro-Vision™ and set of Pro-Values™:

Pro-Vision™: Love God, Love others, Forgive.

Pro-Values™: **H**ave a heart for God's Children
Express gratitude for God's goodness
Love God, Love Others
Praise God for His grace
Enjoy God's creatures and creation
Remove my sins by your power and mercy, God, teach me, heal me, and comfort me.

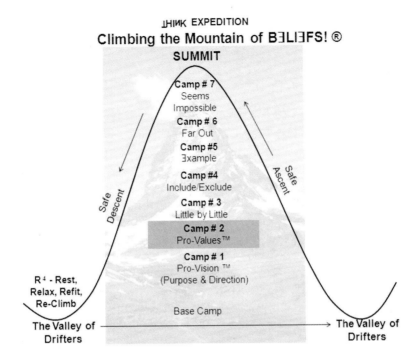

Chapter 3

Improving Little by Little

"A little sleep, a little slumber, a little folding of the hands to rest –"   Proverbs 6:10

Improving

Little by Little

3rd Level of Change - Doing Things Better

Camp 3

The Story of Daniel and Not Eating at the King's Table paraphrased from Daniel 1:1-16

Daniel and three of his friends from Jerusalem were captured and brought to the King's court in Babylon. The men were to eat from the King's table, but Daniel chose to eat differently. He requested that the four eat only vegetables and drink only water for ten days.

Then there would be a determination as to who appeared healthier. Daniel and his friends were healthier after the ten day trial.

We are at Camp 3 – the 3rd Level of Change – Improvement. How does one improve? We improve little by little – the "L" in B3 LI3 FS!® stands for "Little by Little".

Good habits are hard to make and easy to break. Bad habits are easy to make and hard to break.

Dr. Maxwell Maltz wrote a book in 1960 entitled, <u>Psycho-Cybernetics: A New Technique for Using Your Subconscious Power</u>. Dr. Maltz was a plastic surgeon in the days when it wasn't the rage to have different body parts "redesigned" or "re-engineered" to make a person prettier or more attractive.

In his book he described performing surgeries on patients who had been disfigured through accidents (in those days there were no safety glass in vehicles, no seat belts, no airbags, and no retractable steering wheels). Dr. Maltz stated, "Following plastic surgery it takes about 21 days for the average patient to get used to his new face."

Patients who still "saw" themselves as still being disfigured, even though they were doing well, did not adjust to the new image that had been created for them. This fact reminds me of two things. One, mentally the patients could not "see" themselves as being healed after the accident. They could not get over that hurdle. And two, it reminds me of the story of Daniel. Others had to "see" the results of the eating and drinking habits to believe the outcome. People get better little by little. It doesn't happen overnight. People have to "see" that they are getting better before the fact is real.

Growing and Changing

If we are going to grow, we need to change some old habits, beliefs, and thought patterns. We have to be willing to take some positive risks in order to grow in our lives.

That is why diets don't work. The first three letters in the word "diet" spell what? DIE. What do people "die to" when they go on a diet?

They die to the foods and beverages that got them in a rut of being overweight. When they get back down to a weight they wanted to achieve, how do they typically celebrate? Often they celebrate by going back to eating the food and drinking the beverages that got them in trouble in the first place.

Sometimes people can gain and lose and regain upwards of 400 to 500 of same pounds in their lifetime trying out new diets.

However, diets don't work because we go back to our old habits rather than continuing on with new ones.

When we are going to attempt a change in our lives, we have to realize that it takes time to adjust to this new change as with the surgery. When we get pressed, we typically go back to our old ways as with dieting - just like before.

In order to get better <u>know</u> your beliefs. For example, when I was playing high school football, my **B**elief was that you would not be the athlete you could be if you also drank alcoholic beverages.

My **R**ule was, if I went to a party and no one was drinking, I would stay at the party. If, on the other hand, some people showed up with alcohol, I'd leave. That would be my **A**ction.

More About Diets

When people go on a diet, they typically don't change their **B**eliefs about food or beverages. They don't really change their **R**ules – they change only for a short period of time. What they do change are their **A**ctions – but again only until they lose the weight they want and then they start eating and drinking what they ate before. They gain all the weight back and perhaps more the next time, which is the yo-yo effect.

Diets don't work. In order to make a lifestyle change, **B**eliefs have to change, then **R**ules have to change, and then and only then will **A**ctions change.

Good habits are *hard to make* <u>and easy to break</u>. **Bad habits are** *easy to make* <u>and hard to break</u>.

Beliefs, Rules, and Actions in My Life

Let me share a story as an example of changing **B**eliefs, **R**ules, and **A**ctions that did not turn out well for me. It began with what the great motivational speaker Zig Ziglar used to refer to as "Stinking Thinking."

My father was a career Army officer, and the day after I graduated from high school we left South Carolina to travel to Germany. Germany is noted for many things, one of them is excellent beer.

I had this crazy idea that I wanted to get bigger and attempt to play college football back in America when I returned from Germany. Just to show you how poorly thought-out this plan was, I decided to change my **B**eliefs, **R**ules, and **A**ctions to help the process along.

I decided on the flight over to Germany that I would start drinking German beer to get bigger! Now, how dumb was that? It turned out to be one of the dumbest mistakes I have ever made in my life.

Drinking alcohol radically changed my life…but not for the better. It consumed my life for the next twelve years. I am not proud to write this. It became a destructive path in my life, and I'll describe how I changed in the next chapter.

Goal Achievement

To begin achieving your goals you first have to have some goals. Please take whatever time you need to write down 101 goals you'd like to achieve in your lifetime.

I know, I know. That seems like a lot of goals. I want to relate a story that the current ESPN College Football Analyst Coach Lou Holtz has given me permission to repeat here. In 1967 Coach Holtz was a young unemployed college football coach. His wife had given him a book that focused on thinking big, Coach Holtz wrote down 107 goals that he wanted to accomplish in his life. Some of the goals he included were: 1) to become the head football coach at Notre Dame, 2) fly off the deck of an aircraft carrier, 3) hit a hole-in-one in a golf game, and 4) to win the National Collegiate Football Championship. I was in contact with him thirty years later, and he wrote me a note explaining that he had accomplished 102 of the original 107 goals.

The last five goals that Coach Holtz has not accomplished yet are: 1) he is not a scratch golfer (a very good golfer), 2) he has never run with the bulls in Pamplona, Spain (an annual summer festival), 3) he has not been on an African Safari, 4) he has never owned his own manufacturing firm and 5) he has not learned to speak a foreign language.

Let's pick just one of your goals to focus on as an exercise. When I try to accomplish a goal I focus on three things – **L**ights, **C**amera, and **A**ction, the words a movie director uses.

Over the years I have found this is one of the best ways to get started on actually accomplishing a goal: imagine seeing your goal as a movie.

Lights

The Lights of the goal give you an image of what your goal will look like when you have finished it. The old saying, "If you can't see it, you can't get it," holds true here.

If you're not able to visualize a goal before it takes place, you have a very slim chance of ever accomplishing it. Our mind is like a camera, perhaps your cell phone camera. If you don't take a photograph of something, then you have nothing to show to someone.

You can talk about what you're going to do, but until you can actually describe what it's going to look like to another person, it won't happen. It won't be accomplished.

So, get a clear image of what you are trying to accomplish. I tell my college freshmen that if they can't visualize walking across the stage with a cap and gown, they will never accomplish this goal. You have to see the image as though it had already taken place.

Let me give you another example. Super Bowl XLV (45) was won by the Green Bay Packers over the Pittsburgh Steelers 31-25 in February of 2011. Do you know what the Green Bay Packer's head coach, Mike McCarthy, did the Saturday night prior to the Sunday evening game?

He helped the Green Bay team visualize their win before it ever took place. Coach McCarthy had each player fitted for his own Super Bowl ring the night before the game. I cannot think of a more inspiring way to remember how important it is to visualize a goal before you achieve it.

A lot of people do not have any goals. No goals mean they don't have any expectations; therefore, they figure they won't be disappointed. What a tragic way to live life.

It's important to have a purpose, a sense of positive direction in your life. That's what a Pro-Vision™ can give you – something to keep you on track. Remember how the devil keeps ninety-eight percent of the people in the world under his control? He has them just drift through life every day.

So, having a Pro-Vision™ is one thing. Living it out through the goals in your life is another. Don't let the devil steal your joy in life. Stay focused - become Drift-Free – **See the Lights!**

Camera

Now, let's move on to the second part of achieving a goal – the **C**amera. Instant replay has become such an integral part of sports to see if the recording of the event actually shows, beyond a doubt, that the player or the ball was in or out of the line according to the rules of the game.

That's the way you should treat the presence of a camera in your life. You need to keep score of your life on a daily basis. You need to be able to answer this question at the end of each day, "Did I win or did I lose today?"

Who is keeping score? You are keeping score! For example, if you wrote down that you wanted to be a better student as a goal, how will you keep score of this goal? Being a better student does not answer the question "How?" How will you keep score of being a better student?

You need to ask yourself this question at the end of the day, "Did I win or lose today in my quest to be a better student?" It's fairly simple, a yes or a no will answer your question.

Then you can plan your strategy for tomorrow. What are you going to do differently tomorrow to accomplish your goal? Remember, how long does it take to make a habit change? That's right, twenty-one days…minimum! And when you mess up and fall back into an old habit, you have to start counting the 21 days all over again. Better get started now!

Doing what you've always done will only bring you the results you currently have. To accomplish something different, you have to do something different. There is no other way around it.

The old phrase GIGO still applies, too – garbage in, garbage out. If you want to have a different outcome, you have to start with a different input. Good in, good out. Or better yet, God In, God Out!

Action

Do you know what a dream is? I have heard it described as a goal without a date. That makes perfect sense.

The third and final phase of goal accomplishment is **A**ction. In order to achieve something worthwhile in your life you have to write down a specific month, day, and year you want to accomplish this particular goal. Write the goal on two 3 x 5 cards. You keep one card. Give the other to a trusted friend.

Give it to someone you can trust to be an encourager to you, not a discourager. Have him or her check with you each day to see how you are coming along with the attainment of your goal.

On separate 8.5 X 11 sheets of lined paper write down 101 achievement goals you'd like to accomplish in your life. It took me four pages to write my 101 goals.

If you don't get started, you'll never make that movie. Remember, **Lights, Camera, and Action!**

Level 3 Level of Fear: Catastrophizing

Level 3 is the Level of Fear of <u>Catastrophizing</u>. It is the fear of things getting worse. It is seeing only the worst case.

To overcome the fear of expecting the worst, we should focus on positive results and not become overwhelmed with the fear itself.

Let's prepare to climb to Camp 4.

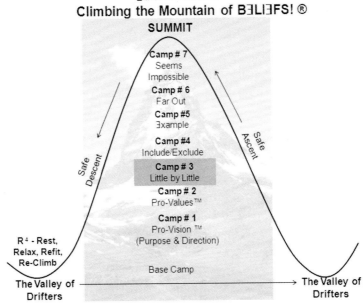

Chapter 4

What Can We Do Without?

"For physical training is of some value, but godliness has value for all things, holding promise for both the present life and the life to come." 1 Timothy 4:8

4th Level of Change – Do Away With Things
Camp 4
Include/Exclude

The Parable of the Sower and Seeds paraphrased from Matthew 13:3-23

Jesus shared the parable about a farmer who sowed his seed. The seeds fell in three different places: rocky soil, among the thorns, and good soil. Only the good soil produced a crop – many times over. He spoke in parables because they only made sense to those who knew Christ.

What does this parable mean? In this chapter we will look at doing away with things that will not produce good results. What is Christ doing away with in this parable? Sowing seeds in good soil would certainly have more effective results than leaving them to dry and wither in rocks and weeds.

Let me ask you a leading question, "How many of the Ten Commandments found in Exodus 20:1-17 are written or expressed with negative words?" What is God telling us to do away with? Each of the negative commands will protect us in life.

"You shall have no other gods before me.

You shall not make for yourself an image in the form of anything in heaven above or on the earth beneath or in the waters below.

You shall not misuse the name of the LORD your God.

You shall not murder.

You shall not commit adultery.

You shall not steal.

You shall not give false testimony against your neighbor.

You shall not covet."

Only two of the Ten Commandments are written as a positive command:

"Remember the Sabbath day by keeping it holy.

Honor your mother and father that your days may be long upon the earth."

When I read Rolf Smith's 4th Level of Change, this is the first thing I thought: Eight of the Commandments are written in a negative manner and only two are stated in a positive manner. In other words, what can you do away with or give up in your life that will have a positive impact on your life?

Our Lord gave these Commandments. They are not suggestions that one can take or leave. They are the laws. He is like the father who protects his children from themselves.

We are continuing to climb the Mountain of **B3 LI3 FS!®**. We are at Camp 4 – the 4th Level of Change. I have included the letter "I" here to remind me that the 4th Level is asking the question, "What do I Include and what do I exclude?

Include/Exclude

Since 2001, I have been walking our big dog early in the morning to make sure he gets enough exercise. I walk Buster right after I do my Bible study early in the morning and before I go work out at the wellness center. When I'm on a trip away from our home, Buster never disturbs Zoe Ann early in the morning. In fact, he never bothers her to go on a walk while I'm gone, ever!

Once I get home, he's ready to go out again the next morning. We walk the same area each morning, but Buster loves it because a lot of other creatures have covered the area during the previous 24 hours, so it's always new territory to him…every day. Same ground, new aromas, new smells, new territory.

One morning when Buster and I were walking, our Lord put this thought in my head: What I do for Buster is what our Lord does for us. Buster knows he has to be on a leash when we go out. I know that our Lord has given me the Ten Commandments to follow daily to be on a protective leash.

Drifters would say these Commandments are restrictions – it doesn't allow us to live a "free" life. Those who have become Drift-Free would say it gives them great freedom to follow the Lord.

Once in a while Buster used to get carried away, and when our garage door was up or we opened the front door he would bolt out into the front yard. He would run down the street "free" as he could be. However, Buster didn't know what a vehicle traveling down our street might do to him. We did.

So we yelled at Buster to stop. He would stop quickly and put his tail between his legs and just wait for me beside the street. He knew he had done something wrong, and in his own way, he appeared to be asking for forgiveness.

I'd pat him on the head and then we'd go back to the house. When Buster runs in the back yard he is free to run anywhere, but he is…inside the fence.

It's that way with our Lord, too. He knows what's best for us. He wants to protect us, but He also gives us the free will to roam. Roaming, like drifting, will get us in trouble. I know. I have done it many times.

The Ten Commandments are there for a reason not as a suggestion of what we might do, but absolutely what we need to do to follow Christ and be safe. Eight of the Ten Commandments are things we need to stop doing – to do without.

It reminds me of the sins in my life. When we start down a particular path, we don't think of the consequences. We think of the fun we're having, not the price we'll pay for the fun.

Sin will take us further down a particular path than we can anticipate. Sin will cost us more than we can imagine. And, sin always has longer lasting consequences that we think it might.

That's the way it is with Buster. As long as he's on the leash or running around in the fenced-in backyard, he's safe. When he decides it's more fun to run without a leash, he finds himself in an unsafe environment.

Remember my ill conceived decision to start drinking when I moved to Germany as a freshman in college? Here's the rest of the story:

When I was accepted at the University of Maryland in Munich, West Germany, I felt like old Buster must feel when he goes out on his own. I was free. I could do anything I wanted to – no restrictions.

The dormitory restrictions were there for a purpose, but, of course, they didn't apply to me. Was I ever wrong! I developed a horrible habit of drinking until I passed out. It was a great form of escape from the cares of life. Excessive drinking was a part of my life until I was thirty years old!

At twenty-eight I became a Christian in Pastor Bill Solomon's church office in Irmo, South Carolina, on August 6th, 1975.

No whistles went off in Bill's office. I didn't feel any different. I didn't even tell Zoe Ann I had become a Christian – very sad, indeed. Nine days later, on August 15th, Zoe Ann's mother died after a long battle with breast cancer.

I got a Bible out and was trying to find a passage of Scripture that might be of comfort to Zoe Ann. But I didn't know where to begin. I wasn't much comfort to her.

Over the next two years I really didn't make any dramatic changes in my life. I went to church on Sunday, but I wasn't active in the church at all – you know the routine – give an hour on Sunday and you are covered for the week

– how sad. As human beings we have a way of rationalizing everything, and that's what I did with my life and drinking.

I rationalized that since the first miracle that Jesus ever performed was turning water into wine (John 2:1-11) at a wedding feast, I could just keep right on drinking. And I did.

Two years later, Pastor Solomon's sermon was on 1 Corinthians 10:31, "*So whether you eat or drink or whatever you do, do it all for the glory of God.*"

At the end of the sermon, he pulled an empty beer can out of a paper bag, raised the can above his head and asked us to remember the next time we had an alcoholic beverage to praise our Lord with it and then drink the beverage.

Have you ever had the wind knocked out of you? I have, playing football, and it's no fun. You feel like you're going to die; you can't catch your breath. It's a real panicky feeling.

That's how I felt sitting in the congregation that morning. I knew I needed to do something about my drinking. There were lots of people in attendance that morning, but I felt like our Lord was speaking specifically to me.

After the service, Zoe Ann asked me about the sermon. I told her and also told her that I needed to do something about my drinking. To her great credit, she did not <u>tell</u> me what to do; instead, she asked me, "What are you going to do?"

I had lots of friends at the time that I partied with, including my three younger brothers. There was over $800 worth of alcohol in the house at the time – I always wanted to be ready to party – I was a Drifter, for sure!

First, I thought I'd call my brothers up and let them come over and purchase what they wanted from the stock – I needed to get my money back, didn't I? Second, I thought I would just give it to them. And then, third, I thought, hey, I'm the oldest, I need to lead here, so I decided to pour all the contents down the drain in the kitchen. And that's what I did. As I recall, it took a long time that day.

For weeks afterward, whenever we turned the spigot on in our kitchen, the place smelled like a brewery! April 10th, 1977, was as the last date I consumed any alcoholic beverage.

If we are going to grow as a Christian, we must learn to listen to our Lord and make some decisions on what not to do. In other words, have a Stop Doing List as well as a To Do List.

This is what this chapter is all about. I have been inspired by Dr. Jim Collins, the Stanford professor, who has authored such best selling books as <u>Built to Last</u>, <u>Good to Great</u>, and <u>Great by Choice</u>. He makes a "Stop Doing List" the cornerstone of his New Year's Resolutions.

What is our Lord asking you to "stop doing"? Listen carefully to what He is saying. Do it now. Write what He is asking you to give up here. Add them to your 101 achievement goals sheets.

I like to put negative words in a positive light. It helps me to stay focused. Years ago the great motivational speaker, Zig Ziglar, asked the question, "Why is it that when we are giving directions to someone we always tell people to go to the stop light? Why don't we tell them to go to the go light?"

That always stuck with me. I even came up with a saying of my own. Instead of having deadlines for things to be done, why not have lifelines? It's the same date, just put in a positive light. It makes it more agreeable sounding to me and my way of thinking.

So, instead of having a "Don't List," why not have a "Freely Give Up Achievement Goals List?" Sounds good to me.

Instead of thinking of eight of the Ten Commandments in a negative light, why not see them in a positive light?

"Have one God

Be Image-Free

Be Profanity-Free

Be Murder-Free

Be Adultery-Free

Be Steal-Free

Be Honest

Be Covet-Free."

Level 4 Level of Fear: Holding On

Level 4 is the Level of Fear of Holding On. It is the Fear of Letting Go. We focus on the 80% that only brings 20% of the value. We Fear if we stop doing something, it will be a mistake. We have a Just-in-Case Fear.

To overcome this Level of Fear focus our efforts on the 20% that brings 80% of the value in our lives.

Let's make a strong effort to climb to the next camp – Camp 5.

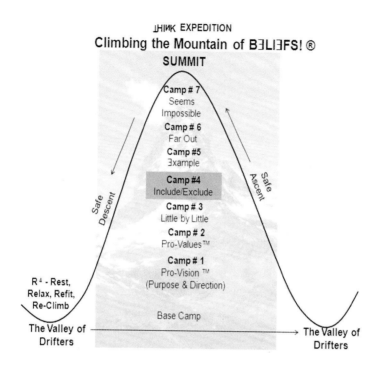

Chapter 5

Do What Others Have Done

"As iron sharpens iron, so one person sharpens another."
                                                        Proverbs 27:17

Ǝ - Example
Level 5 of Change
Copy, Copy, Copy
Camp 5

Worry, Worry Not!

A Bible Story paraphrased from Matthew 6:25-34

Jesus told us not to worry…about anything. This is exactly the opposite of what the devil wants us to do. He wants us to worry all the time. It wastes a lot of energy, not to mention time. Worrying will not add one single hour to our lives. We continue to be Drifters – the 98% of the people in the world who worry.

The best advice our Lord gives is to first seek His kingdom and His righteousness, and everything else will be given to us. Our Lord knows exactly what we need before we need it or even think about needing it.

We are at Camp 5 – This is where the second "Ǝ" is used in climbing the Mountain of **BƎ LIƎ FS!®**. The backward "Ǝ" reminds me of the word Example. Or as Col. Smith says, "Copy, Copy, Copy!"

Benchmarking as a term has been around for a long time. Businesses use this practice a lot. It is another way of saying copy. Copy the best practices from another company or industry to help your own company.

When I first started the Coach's Corner in 1995, I had an opportunity to travel to Orlando, Florida, and take a couple of courses from the Disney Institute. Disney is not gullible enough to give away all their magic, but they are willing, for a fee, to share some of their insights of what has worked for them over the years. It's a grand experience.

I also attended a benchmarking seminar that the Ritz-Carlton Hotel Company held at its Buckhead facility in Atlanta, Georgia. While there, I was able to learn from the Ritz-Carlton Hotels how they won the Malcolm Baldrige National Quality Award, twice, in 1992 and again in 1999.

I also attended the Milliken & Company Pursuit of Excellence Quality Seminar in Spartanburg, South Carolina, in 1993 to discover how they won the Malcolm Baldrige National Quality Award in 1989. This was only the second year that the Baldrige Award had been awarded. Roger Milliken (1915-2010) was the grandson of the co-founder of the textile giant Milliken & Company. Roger saw to it that the company was run with quality as the "buzz word" for the company.

The Malcolm Baldrige National Quality Award

Malcolm Baldrige (1922-1987) grew up on a ranch in the Midwest. His business career was focused mainly in the manufacturing arena, and he became the Secretary of Commerce under President Ronald Reagan.

An unfortunate horse riding accident at a rodeo caused Secretary Baldrige to be killed in 1987. Congress created The National Quality Award to honor Mr. Baldrige's service to America. In 2010 the award was changed to The Baldrige Performance Excellence Program.

A company has to apply to be considered for the award. Once the application has been processed and the fee paid, a team of judges spends months reviewing the particulars of the company as they relate to the quality standards of the award. It is a very competitive process. This award is a great honor for the companies that win; they become benchmark performers.

The Deming Prize

Have you ever heard of a man by the name of W. Edwards Deming? He has a famous quality award named after him…in of all places - Japan. Dr. Deming (1900-1993) was a statistical expert. During World War II Dr. Deming and others were responsible for the huge increase in production of war material in the United States.

The Total Quality Management imitative that Dr. Deming taught made a major difference in how things got built in America during the war.

General Douglas MacArthur (1880-1964) was put in charge of Japan after World War II with the express purpose of bringing democracy to the Japanese people. Between 1945 and 1951 he helped bring about changes unheard of in Japan. General MacArthur also invited Dr. Deming to come to Japan to help teach the Japanese industrial leaders the finer points of Total Quality Management in 1950.

The Japanese industrial leaders were so impressed with Dr. Deming's teachings that they created a Deming Prize for exhibiting the highest quality in their field. Japan's industry made a huge paradigm shift to Total Quality. By 1980 Japan's quality effort had surpassed that of the United States.

The National Broadcasting Corporation (NBC) aired a two hour program on, "If Japan Can...Why Can't We?" I still remember watching that television show one evening in 1980. It revolutionized the way America's industry looked at itself. The big automakers in America wanted to know where they could find this "Deming" fellow. At 80, he was retired and living in Washington, D.C., not too far from the White House.

Everyone wanted exclusive rights to Deming. They wanted Dr. Deming's total quality principles taught only to their own people. He would have none of that and proceeded to teach anyone who wanted to learn his statistical approach to quality, regardless of their background or profession.

Dr. Deming was so successful; he was teaching one of his seminars just weeks before he died at age 93!

The Deming Prize in Japan was part of the push to have the Malcolm Baldrige Quality Award created here in America. His life is still having an impact on today's industrial society around the world.

Both the Deming Prize and The Baldrige Performance Excellence Program are two excellent examples of how benchmarking or copying can make a difference in the life of a company. Individuals from companies all over the world go to these company winners and copy, copy, copy.

Let me change the focus on benchmarking from industry to individuals.

In 1983 I met Pastor Randy Riddle at the Wesminister Presbyterian Church in Conway, SC. He introduced me to the concept of keeping a daily prayer sheet to pray for others. I still use that concept today and have logged almost 600 sheets of prayer requests. This is an example of how I used the idea of copy, copy, copy.

I pray over the current year's prayer requests while the others are in big binders.

Whenever I lose my focus, I re-read those earlier prayer requests and review how our Lord has been working in my life and the lives of others. It is a real blessing to go back to 1983 to see how our Lord has answered so many prayers.

Think of something someone is doing that you admire. What is it that you'd like to copy?

How can you make what another person is doing fit your life? What specifically will it take to use this concept to make it your own?

How can you suspend judgment on this new idea before you even try it out? Be very specific in describing how you are going to implement this new "benchmark" in your life?

Remember, how many days does it take to make a habit change? That's right, 21 days. Start counting today as Day One of your new habit.

Write the date down on your new habit change, and describe the habit here.

Mile Markers

Another concept we can discuss is the Mile Marker approach to copying things. In order to accomplish what you want to accomplish for our Lord, you need to see how you are growing.

Do you remember when you were a child and you were on a road trip with your parents? In a bored state you might have asked, "Are we there yet?" Someone might have said, "A little while longer."

To someone who has no sense of time, "A little while longer," has no relevance, but if you knew how to count the Mile Markers on the side of the road you could have a better sense of time and distance. You need to come up with a way of keeping track of your own progress as you copy what others have done before you.

In Chapter 8 we will get into God's Goal Achievement Program. One of the ways Mile Markers can be used is to keep track of both short and long term goals and their achievement.

Level 5 Level of Fear: Self-Doubt

Level 5 is the Level of Fear of Self-Doubt. There is the Fear of not being physically able to accomplish the task at hand. There is the Fear of copying the wrong thing or Fear of copying the right thing the wrong way. There is always the ever present Fear of being laughed at! The Fear of Criticism and the Fear of Self are also distressing fears.

The best way to overcome this Fear is: If you can't physically do it, find someone else on your team that can do it. Employ the help of others on your team to have a buddy system. Have team members be responsible for each other. Encourage one another. Do not be a discourager. Don't laugh at others. Lift them up.

Let's climb to Camp 6.

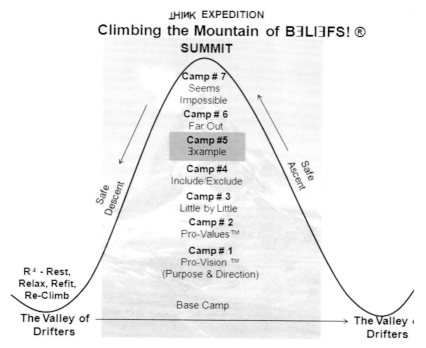

Chapter 6

What's FAR OUT?

"Now then, my children, listen to me; blessed are those who keep my ways.
^{33} Listen to my instruction and be wise; do not disregard it.
^{34} Blessed are those who listen to me, watching daily at my doors, waiting at my doorway. ^{35} For those who find me find life and receive favor from the LORD. ^{36} But those who fail to find me harm themselves; all who hate me love death."   Proverbs 8:32-36

"F" - Far Out
6th Level of Change
Do Things That Haven't Been Done
Ask "Why Not?"
Do What Others Are Not Doing

Camp 6

We are getting closer to the summit of the Mountain of **BƎ LIƎ FS!®**. We are climbing toward Camp 6. Only one more camp to go and we'll have safely and successfully reached the Summit. Camp 6 is where Level 6 takes place – Do what others are not doing.

The "**F**" in **BƎ LIƎ FS!®** reminds me of "**Far Out!**". It is a way of saying you are cool; you are doing what other people are not doing or you are a cool dude.

Before we introduce this next Scripture, a little explanation is in order. In Biblical times a Samaritan was an outcast. They were untouchable people – an Israelite just didn't associate with them in any way. Sounds like some people we know today, doesn't it?

"When a Samaritan woman came to draw water, Jesus said to her, "Will you give me a drink?" The Samaritan woman said to him, "You are a Jew and I am a Samaritan woman. How can you ask me for a drink?" John 4:7-9.

It was the custom of the day that a man was not to speak to a woman not related to him. Both Jesus and the Samaritan woman knew that Jesus, as a Jew, was not to speak to a Samaritan woman...ever! This situation had even more dire consequences.

Now, let's look at a different situation involving a Samaritan man.

The Parable of the Good Samaritan paraphrased from Luke 10: 25-37

Jesus told the parable surrounding the greatest commandment: "Love the Lord your God with all your heart and with all your soul and with all your strength and with all your mind'; and, 'Love your neighbor as yourself."

Robbers robbed a man and left him for dead on the side of the road. A priest came down the road, but crossed over on the other side so as not to have to deal with the untouchable.

Another man came down the road and saw the robbed man and chose to pass by on the other side of the road.

A Samaritan man came down the road and stopped to help the wounded man. He took the man to a hotel and paid for the man's treatment.

Then Jesus asked who of the three was a neighbor to the wounded man?

Although the next Scripture reading does not involve a Samaritan, the lesson is similar.

The Parable of the Lost Son paraphrased from Luke 10:11-32

Jesus spoke of another parable. A man had two sons. His youngest son wanted his money from his father's estate right then. That was not the custom, but the father agreed to give his son the money.

The prodigal (extravagant) son spent all of his father's money on wine, women, and the good life. One day he ran out of the money and couldn't get a job. He was able to feed the pigs where he lived – the pigs ate better than the boy did.

So the boy went home as a beaten man. His father saw him down the road and welcomed the boy home. The boy's older brother was not happy.

As the oldest son, he would inherit the majority of the money and land. He had been a faithful son, but now the father wanted to throw a party for his lost son who had returned home.

In my office I have two prints of two paintings that I enjoy looking at daily. Both paintings are done by Dutch artists, but from two different eras.

"The Good Samaritan" was painted by Vincent van Gogh in 1890. The second painting is entitled, "The Return of the Prodigal Son" by Rembrandt. It was completed sometime in the 1660s. The two paintings inspire and chastise me daily.

I know what I should do in different situations, and I know that I don't do what I need to do every time. It is very humbling.

As Paul wrote in a letter to the Romans, *"For I do not do the good I want to do, but the evil I do not want to do—this I keep on doing."* (Romans 7:19)

In each of the preceding parables, a man stood up for his fellow man. Parables were always used as teaching stories. In the case of the Samaritan man, he did what others were not willing to do – he helped the man who was robbed and paid for the care of the beaten man.

In the case of the younger son, the "prodigal" or extravagant son, the father was so happy to see him, he wanted to throw a party for his safe return. The older son was upset that his father would even recognize his younger brother. He had been the faithful one all the time and no one ever threw him a party. The older brother thought that the treatment was unfair, but the father stood up for the younger brother.

You are a unique creation by God. There has never has been nor will there ever be a person exactly like you. That's great news. Now, go back to your personal Pro-Vision™ and set of Pro-Values™ and listen to what our Lord is telling you what you can do for Him that no one else can do in His kingdom. Remember: we are the two per-centers of the world – we have a purpose and a sense of direction! We are Drift-Free. We can do things no one else is doing.

What can you do that no one else is doing? Write it here.

If it is so unique, why aren't you doing it now?

What can we do of significance that no one else is built to do?

Add this response to your 101 Achievement Goals List.

Level 6 Level of Fear: Normalcy

Level 6 is the Level of Fear of Normalcy. We Fear being Different. We Fear Being Noticed. We continue to Fear being laughed at. We Fear being rejected. We Fear we are not following Tradition. We Fear trying things that might not work. We Fear that we might fall off trying. We Fear the unexpected. We Fear getting hurt. We Fear being exposed.

To overcome these Fears we will throw two things at them: 1). In the Bible God says 365 times "Fear Not!" and 2). Joshua 1:9 says," Have I not commanded you? Be strong and courageous. Do not be afraid; do not be discouraged, for the LORD your God will be with you wherever you go." Aren't these powerful messages? Take time to read them again.

Let's climb up to the last camp and beyond to the summit.

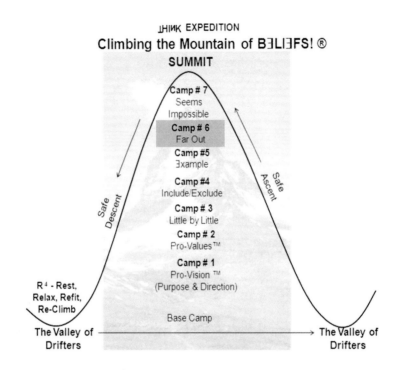

Chapter 7

This Is Impossible!

"*Even though I walk through the darkest valley, I will fear no evil, for you are with me; your rod and your staff, they comfort me.*"   Psalm 23:4

The 7th Level of Change
Seems Impossible

Camp 7 and the Summit

The Walls of Jericho paraphrased from Joshua 6:1-27

God told Joshua that the city of Jericho would be delivered into the hands of the Israelites. He was going to deliver the king and all his men and the inhabitants of Jericho in an unusual way.

God asked Joshua and his men to march around the walled city once a day for six days. On the seventh day, they were to march around the outside of the city seven times.

They would also have the seven priests blow their ram horns. With a long blast on the horns, the Israelite army was instructed to shout out. And the walls came tumbling down.

Our team is just below Camp 7 – the last camp! We are about to make our way up to the Summit of the Mountain **BƎ LIƎ FS!®**. How does it feel to almost be at the top?

There are lots of challenges still in front of us and below us to conquer. In fact, for as long as we live on this earth, we'll be in one of three positions when it comes to challenges: just coming out of a challenge, in the middle of one, or about to start a new one.

It doesn't get any easier as we climb higher – the air is thinner, we are almost exhausted, we are hungry, we are cold, our muscles can hardly get us to pick up our feet for another step.

We have 6 Levels of Changes that we have mastered along the way. Now, we come to Level 7 – **Seems Impossible**. It **S**eems **I**mpossible to go on up on to the Summit of the Mountain of **BƎ LIƎ FS!®** . This is the "**S**" in **BƎ LIƎ FS!®**.

We have come so far, and yet, we're not at the Summit. What must we do? We must call on our Lord to give us the wisdom, the discernment and the strength to carry on. We must do the impossible as a team – God's team.

Let's Review

At Level 1 we learned to daily live out our Pro-Vision™. To live out our Pro-Visions™ gives us a sense of purpose and a positive direction. That sense of Pro-Vision™ helps us to be two per-centers in the world. We are not Drifters. We are not like the 98% of the people in the world. No, we are "Drift-Freers".

At Level 2 we learned to rely on our Pro-Values™ to keep us on the right path before our Lord. We need to focus daily on what lies ahead of us, not looking backward, but striving forward in our expedition.

At Level 3 we examined ways to improve our goals and our Achievement Goals List. Over time, we will never run out of goals. There will always be something more we can do.

At Level 4 we learned to create our "Freely Give Up Achievement List"! What are we striving to stop doing – to focus on what we do best? We cannot be all things to all people. Let us do what we do best.

Level 5 is to benchmark what others are doing. We copied the successful ones who have journeyed on before us. No sense in having to re-invent the wheel, if the wheel already exists.

Level 6 is to do what no one else is doing. What does that look like? What can we uniquely do in God's Kingdom that no one else can do? What can we do of significance that no one else is built to do?

Yes, it looks impossible, but if you could do it, what would it look like? What would need to happen to make it a reality? Do that!

And now we are at the top – we have climbed to the Summit of the Mountain of B3 LI3 FS!®. The view up here is indescribable. The air is thin, and we are so cold and hungry and tired. We made it! But we also know that we can't stay here. We can't live here.

Erik Weihenmayer, co author of The Adversity Advantage: Turning Everyday Struggles into Everyday Greatness says, "Adversity is the parent of our possibilities." We have come so far. When faced with an impossible situation, don't give up. Keep going.

We will be returning to the Valley of Drifters, where ninety-eight percent of the world lives. They are the ones who drift through life. We must share with them about becoming Drift-Free.

The walls of Jericho were famous for being impregnable. The walls were not built as a traditional wall that you might imagine around a castle. These walls were an engineering marvel. There were a series of walls built at an ever increasing angle and thickness, so that at the top of the wall, it was impossible to climb or attack.

It seemed so impossible to the human mind that the walls could ever be breached. Our Lord's ways, are not our ways and having faith in what our Lord said made the difference - all the difference. And the walls came tumbling down!

What we want to do is remember what we saw and how we can safely descend back down the Mountain **BƎ LIƎ FS!**® and take another team of climbers to the top again.

When we hike in the Valley of Drifters, we must remember the 4 R's: Rest, Relax, Refit and Re-Climb.

In order to be well enough to take another expedition back up to the Mountain of **BƎ LIƎ FS!**® we have to be #1 well rested. #2 we also need to take some time to relax and reflect on what we accomplished in safely climbing and descending the mountain. #3 we need to refit ourselves for the climb – we must be prepared for the harshness and the challenges and the adversities of the elements in tackling the journey again. And #4 we must take care to re-climb the mountain with others. Doing it once is not enough. We need to take others with us, so that they, too, can become two per-centers and Drift-Free.

I took the photograph of The Matterhorn pictured on the front cover of the book in 2008 when Zoe Ann and I went to Germany on a Rhine River cruise. We started in Amsterdam, Holland, and took a large river boat all the way up the Rhine River to Basel, Switzerland. From there we took buses and trains to the Swiss town of Zermatt, Switzerland, at the base of The Matterhorn.

The Matterhorn is over 14,000 feet above sea level, and it sits between the borders of Switzerland and Italy.

In addition to the two prints hanging in my office of the two Dutch painters, I also have a painting of the Matterhorn I purchased while on the observation post overlooking the Matterhorn.

The Matterhorn was successfully climbed for the very first time in 1865. Seven climbers made it to the top on that first climb, but only four descended successfully. Over the years over 500 people have died trying to climb the Matterhorn. It is a difficult ascent and descent.

Climbing to the top is only half of the battle. Successfully descending a mountain also takes courage and planning and being careful. In order to make a successful climb, one must descend successfully, too.

To do that, we have to ask ourselves some questions:

1) What is impossible to do today, but…if you could do it, what would it look like?

2) Wouldn't it be amazing if…If what, what would that be?

3) What would take a miracle to occur to make it happen?

4) Go back to your 101 achievement goals, and ask, "What are your three biggest Lifetime Goals?

    A)

    B)

    C)

5) What are your three biggest goals for the next three years?

    A)

    B)

    C)

6) If you had 6 months to live, what would be your three biggest goals?

    A)

    B)

    C)

My three biggest goals for all 6 of these questions are the same. It is to see three people I am close to come to have a personal relationship with our Lord. That is what I am living for.

Additionally, I pray for my children, their spouses, and my grandchildren daily. I pray for Christian mates. I pray our Lord will allow me to live long enough to see my grandchildren graduate from college.

Congratulations on successfully and safely climbing the Mountain of **BƎ LIƎ FS!**®

Level 7 Level of Fear is Disbelief – The Fear of the Unknown.

Level 7 is the Level of Fear of Disbelief – The Fear of the Unknown. We have a Fear of not having a basis of comparison. We have a Fear of Believing. We have a Fear of not being able to do to the task at hand. We have a Fear of Total Failure. We have a Fear of the sum of all Fears.

To overcome this Fear again we draw on our Lord's words in John 16:33, *"I have told you these things, so that in me you may have peace. In this world you will have trouble. But take heart! I have overcome the world."*

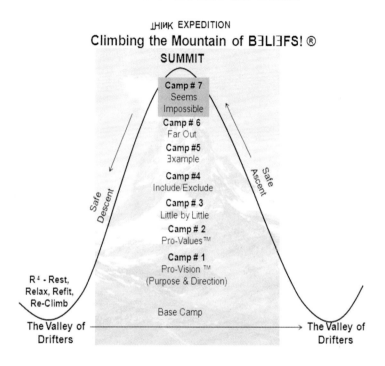

Now it is time to look at Achievement Goals from God's perspective.

Chapter 8

God's Goals

"I press on toward the goal to win the prize for which God has called me heavenward in Christ Jesus." Philippians 3:14

The Story of Noah and the Flood paraphrased from Genesis 6:9-22

God said that Noah was a righteous man. Noah and his wife had three sons and the sons were married.

God saw that the world was very corrupt. So corrupt that the only way the earth could be cleansed of this scourge was to flood the entire earth.

To that end God instructed Noah to construct a triple decked ark made of cypress wood to God's exacting dimensions. God made a covenant with Noah and his family that they would be saved. No one else would be saved.

Noah was instructed to gather up two of every kind of creature on the earth. He was to gather food and water for all aboard.

Explicit About the Instructions

Throughout the Bible our God has demonstrated that He is a precise and accurate God. He didn't tell Noah to build an ark anyway he wanted to. God instructed Noah to use a very precise type of wood, and God even gave Noah the exact measurements of the ark and how to make the vessel watertight.

We must also remember that up until this time, it had never rained on the earth - ever! The water needed by man and other creatures on the earth was provided by God through underground springs. For many years, as Noah and his family built the ark, the people of the earth laughed at him. But Noah continued to build the ark as instructed.

Noah listened to what God had said to him, and he responded. He responded not with complaints and doubt; he responded by doing exactly what God asked him to do. No questions asked.

This is exactly how our Lord would have us respond to Him today. Noah and his family experienced all 7 Levels of Change in building the ark. They climbed their own Mountain of BƎ LIƎ FS!®.

Can you imagine being asked to build something that no one had ever seen before – an ark to survive a flood of worldwide proportions (to do what seems impossible)? Can you imagine how Noah and his family must have felt knowing that they had to gather up all the creatures on the earth and put them on the ark (to do what no one else is doing)?

Can you imagine gathering up all the food needed to feed all the creatures and storing it inside the ark (to benchmark)? Can you imagine not being able to take any other human beings on the ark (doing away with things)?

Can you imagine God believing you, your wife, your three sons, and their wives will be the ones to improve the stock of mankind on the earth (improving little by little)? Can you imagine God making a covenant with you and your family (being Efficient)? And, finally, can you imagine God allowing you to walk with Him (Being Effective)?

We are talking about having a lot of faith in our God. And that is exactly what Noah and his family did.

Today we live in a world of unimaginable inventions and man-made creations. We live in a world that is desperately wicked and evil. We know that God promised never to bring a world-wide flood again. That doesn't mean He doesn't have other ways of getting our attention.

And let's not forget the devil. He has his own plans about how things ought to be run.

In the midst of all this turmoil, let's look at the 101 goals we have written down. Go through your list and determine which ones are from our Lord and are God driven. Also, go through the goals and determine which ones are from you and are self driven.

Perhaps, if you're like me, your list has shrunk! That's fine. Our Lord will reveal other goals for you to pursue.

Now, let's change gears. Let's look at your goals in a different light. Over the years I have attended seminars and read books on goals and how to achieve them.

One thing that stood out to me was that many of the speakers and writers explained how to look at the goals in our lives as though the goals were slices in a pie. There would be a number of ways of cutting the pie up into different sized wedges.

Our Lord showed me that this is man's way of looking at this issue. But, it's not God's way.

Our Lord showed me a different way to look at our life goals. We should look at life as a wheel. From my research I have found that no one is exactly sure when the wheel was first invented. There is evidence that perhaps a rounded mill stone was used to grind wheat over five thousand years ago.

The Wooden Wheels of Egyptian Chariots

At sometime an enterprising person thought of using wheels to pull a cart. The first time there is a mention of a wheeled chariot in the Bible is when Moses and the Israelites were being pursued by Pharaoh and his Egyptian Army.

Exodus 14: 6-9, and 17-31 paraphrased

The Egyptian Pharaoh took six hundred of his best chariots to bring the Israelites back. Our Lord used this event to demonstrate who was really in charge.

An angel of the Lord's came between the Israelites and the Egyptian Army. Moses stretched out his hand over the Red Sea and it parted! The Israelites walked through the part on dry land.

Moses was instructed to stretch out his hand again over the sea. The entire Egyptian Army was wiped out.

Egyptian chariots had wooden wheels that were made up of six wooden spokes. Through my good friend, John Davidson, the Lord revealed to me that I had been thinking about this concept of the wheel totally backwards! I was still thinking about the wheel as a pie image.

John showed me I needed to be looking at it as a real wooden wheel.

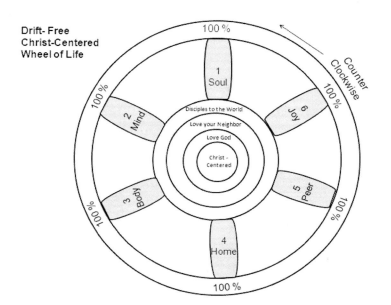

I'd like to ask a question, "Does the earth rotate on its axis in a clock-wise or counter-clockwise direction?" In America many storms travel from the west to the east. When we fly from the west coast toward the east coast we might have a tail wind. The earth rotates on its axis in a counter clockwise direction.

Let's carry this question a little further. "Does the earth's moon revolve around the earth in a clockwise or counter clockwise direction?" It is definitely counter clockwise.

And out even further, "Does the earth revolve around the sun in a clockwise or counter clockwise direction?" Again, it is a counter clockwise direction. I can't tell you why our Lord designed our planets to rotate in this manner, but He did.

It's also interesting to note that many of the races that man has devised for his entertainment are also run in a counter clockwise direction. Typically, the races are run around a track of some dimension and distance – usually an oblong shape. There are horse races, dog races, people races, vehicle races, and many more. The point is that the races are all run counter clockwise (even the Roman Chariot Races from the days of Jesus were run in the Roman Coliseum in a counter clockwise direction)! And the American invented game of baseball has the runners running in a counter clockwise direction.

Our Lord set the earth up in outer space to rotate counter clockwise - twice. We are moving at over 1000 miles per hour around our axis…counter clockwise. And we're moving at over 67,000 miles per hour around the sun. Do you feel the movement? It's amazing how precise our Lord is with numbers. He is, in fact, the ultimate miracle God.

Let's look at one more mathematical fact: "The earth's axis of rotation is tilted at what angle – at what degree?" Give up? The answer is 23.5 degrees. Do you know what would happen if our rotation was off half a degree – either way? That's something to ponder, isn't it?

The God Shaped Hole

I believe we are all born with a "hole" in our heart. As human beings, we spend a lot of our time trying to fill the "hole" up with something that will satisfy our soul. Sometimes we deliberately search for ways to fill up the "hole." Other times we just drift through life, first trying one thing, then another.

There is something that will fill that "hole" in our soul perfectly, but many of us tend to reject it. I know; I have been there. I have searched high and low in my life for just the right thing to fill that "hole."

The only thing that can fill that "hole" is establishing a personal one-on-one relationship with Jesus Christ. Nothing else will do. We are born on this earth with this "hole" in our soul and one of two things occurs:

1). Either we remain as we were born, Drifters with no sense of purpose or direction in our lives. We are the ninety-eight per-centers of all the people who have ever roamed the earth and we have chosen to stay as we were born – Drifters. We chose this path for eternity, as well.

2). The other way is to choose to become a Drift-Free two per-center and to create a definite sense of purpose and direction for our lives. Choosing this path will make all the difference in our lives on this earth.

It has been said that we either are born once and die twice; or we are born twice and die only once. In other words, we have a physical birth, but never enter into a personal relationship with Jesus Christ and our body dies and so does our soul.

Or we have a physical birth and a spiritual birth by choice, and only die once in the physical sense. Our soul goes to heaven.

Our Lord has a plan already laid out for each of us. It is tailor made to fit only our unique design. Or you can follow your own game plan. No one else _can_ do or _will_ do exactly what we are capable of doing. We all have our own game plan. No two game plans are alike.

The Hub

As we look at the diagram of the wooden wheel used in an Egyptian chariot, we can see a central area known as the hub. This hub is like a large hole. What is put into the hole will affect all the spokes of the wheel.

Let's look at the hub of the wooden Egyptian chariot wheel as a representation of a person's Drift-Free Wheel of Life. In the Center is "Christ". Once we have made the choice to follow Christ, then the "hole" in our soul begins to fill up with the Holy Spirit. This "filling" will affect every other part of the spokes in the wheel or all the parts of our lives.

This is different from the conventional way of examining goals in that the "spiritual" side of life is not just another piece of the pie. It is the <u>center</u> of our lives and everything radiates out from that – like the rays of the sun on a beautiful day.

This is how Juliane Smith describes filling the hole in her heart with God.

I Have It All

"I have a Mercedes-Benz and diamond rings,
And Rosenthal china and tons of pretty things.

Someone does my yard, and I have a maid.
Others have worked while I've painted and played.

I have it all!
I have an education; I've read stacks of books.
I have money for clothes to enhance my good looks.

Silk and 600 count sheets touch my skin.
<u>Nothing</u> ugly is allowed in the world that I'm in.

I have it all!

I have a husband who's faithful and children who love me.
I have grand kids and great people on my family tree.

I have my good health.
Dear friends, love and laughter – a true measure of wealth.

I have it all!
I have it all?

Three houses, ten pets, to dream and to pray.

For all that I have, God, all that I can say is thank you and thank you and thank you again.

I'm blessed and I'm loved by you , God, everyday.

The best that I have, God, comes from answering your call.

It's with you in my heart, God, that I truly have it all."

The next two parts of the hub relate to Matthew 22:34-39,

[34]Hearing that Jesus had silenced the Sadducees, the Pharisees got together. [35] One of them, an expert in the law, tested him with this question: [36] "Teacher, which is the greatest commandment in the Law?"

[37] Jesus replied: "'Love the Lord your God with all your heart and with all your soul and with all your mind.' [38] This is the first and greatest commandment. [39] And the second is like it: 'Love your neighbor as yourself.'"

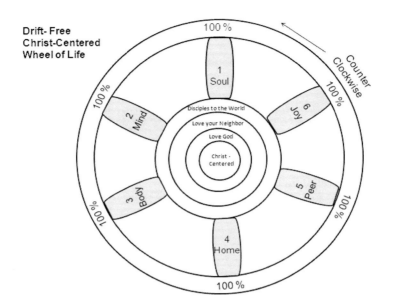

The Pharisee was not referring to the original Ten Commandments that we've already discussed in the chapter on doing away with things. By this time in Jewish history there were over 600 laws that the Jews were expected to keep – these were man-made laws. If Jesus picked any one of the 600 hundred laws it would negate the others. It was a trick question!

Jesus did not hesitate in his response. He said, *"Love the Lord your God with all your heart and with all your soul and with all your mind.* " Back to the wheel diagram, you will see next to the center of the hub is "to Love God." In other words, to love God with 100% of your being.

And next to "Love God" radiates "Love Your Neighbor."

The final part of the hub is "to make disciples of all nations." This is from Matthew 28:18-20,

> "[18] Then Jesus came to them and said, "All authority in heaven and on earth has been given to me. [19] Therefore go and make disciples of all nations, baptizing them in the name of the Father and of the Son and of the Holy Spirit, [20] and teaching them to obey everything I have commanded you. And surely I am with you always, to the very end of the age."

Six Wooden Spokes

Next, we will examine the representation of the six spokes in the wooden Egyptian chariot wheel. The six spokes represent the six areas where we can achieve goals in our lives. Just as our Lord has set the planets to rotate and revolve in a counter clockwise direction, we will move in a counter clockwise manner, as well.

Having that "hole" filled by Christ changes everything. Spoke #1 is where we can examine our "Soul" Achievement Goals.

Observe the two ends of each spoke as they are connected to the outer wheel and the inner hub. Imagine the inner connection showing zero growth and the outer connection of each spoke would represent 100% growth. Place a line on the spoke that represents where you see yourself in your spiritual growth right now between zero and 100%.

Begin with Soul Spoke #1. Place your line through the spoke noting where you think you are between zero and 100%.

Spend some time with our Lord in prayer and listen to what goals He would have you pursue in this Soul Spoke.

Add these to your 101 Achievement Goals List.

Rotating counter clockwise, let's examine Spoke #2. This is your "Mind" Achievement Goals spoke. This is what the Holy Spirit sees in your life. What does this mean?

Jesus Promises Another Helper

In John 14:16-18, Jesus will send another helper, the Holy Spirit, who dwells with you and inside you.

What needs to change? When? How? Why?

What have you been doing to expand your mind (no drugs allowed!)? What books are you reading, or what kind of Internet sites or television entertains you?

Remember the term Garbage In, Garbage Out? Let's change that old common term to, "God In, God Out."

Again, observe that the part of Spoke #2 that is connected inside the hub is at a zero growth and the part of Spoke #2 connected to the outer wheel is at 100% growth. Place a line on the spoke that represents where you see yourself in the growth of your mind right now. Spend some time with our Lord in prayer – just talk to Him - and listen to what goals He would have you pursue.

Add these to your 101 Achievement Goals' List.

Spoke #3 is where we can examine our "Body" Achievement Goals. Do you know how many muscles you have in your body? 639, but who's counting? How about the number of bones? 206.

Your Body is where the Holy Spirit dwells in your life. My questions to you are, "Are you pleased with the way your temple looks and feels?" What needs to change? When? How? Why?

What are you doing about your weight or your exercise program? Are you focusing on healthy choices for food and drink? Are you reducing the distress to your body and getting enough daily rest and relaxation? What about disciplining yourself to do the right things?

Just as you drew a line through the previous spokes, place a line on the Body Spoke that represents where you see yourself in your Body Achievement Goals right now. Spend some time with our Lord in prayer and listen to what goals He would have you pursue.

Add these to your 101 Achievement Goals' List.

Spoke #4 is where we can examine our "Home" Achievement Goals. These are the relationships the Holy Spirit is involved with within our family. My question is, "Are you pleased with these relationships?" What needs to change? When? How? Why?

What are you doing about your love for your family? How much time are you spending with your family? Is what you do for a living in balance with your home life? What about disciplining yourself to do the right things?

Place a line on the spoke that represents where you see yourself in your Home Achievement Goals right now based on zero growth near the hub and 100% growth near the outer wheel. Spend some time with our Lord in prayer and listen to what goals He would have you pursue.

Add these to your 101 Achievement Goals' List.

Spoke #5 is where we can examine our "Peer" Achievement Goals. These are the relationships the Holy Spirit is involved with within your friends and acquaintances. My question is, "Are you pleased with these relationships?" What needs to change? When? How? Why?

What are you doing about your love for your friends? How much time are you spending with your friends? Are your friends bringing you down or building you up? Are you the smartest person in your group? If you are, perhaps it is time to get involved in another group. What about disciplining yourself to do the right things?

Place a line on the spoke that represents where you see yourself in your Peer Achievement Goals right now (zero growth near the hub connection and 100% growth near the outer wheel connection). Spend some time with our Lord in prayer and listen to what goals He would have you pursue. Write them here.

Add these to your 101 Achievement Goals' List.

Spoke #6 is where we can examine our "Joy" Achievement Goals. If you will notice the other five spokes had four letter words associated with each one. The term "Work" has a bad connotation to it. One should "enJOY" what we do for a living – whether it is a fulltime job, a part-time job, a volunteer job, or attending school. These are the relationships the Holy Spirit is involved with others in your life. My question is, "Are you pleased with these relationships?" What needs to change? When? How? Why?

Do you know the difference between happiness and joy? Happiness has to do with "What's Happening?" It is a temporary period of time. It won't last. It relies on the <u>outside world</u> to make one happy. It allows people to Drift to find happiness.

Being joyful has to do with <u>how you are inside</u>. Joyful lasts a long time because it is not dependant on "What's Happening." It depends on the Holy Spirit inside. As the Apostle Paul wrote in Philippians 4:11, *"Not that I speak in regard to need, for I have learned in whatever state I am, to be content."*

What are you doing about how you demonstrate joy in your life? What about disciplining yourself to do the right things?

Place a line on the spoke that represents where you see yourself in your Joy Achievement Goals right now. Remember that zero growth is located near the hub connection and 100% growth is located near the outer wheel connection. Spend some time with our Lord in prayer and listen to what goals He would have you pursue. Write them here.

Add these to your 101 Achievement Goals' List.

All of these Achievement Goals are guided by being Christ-Centered. You are on your way to becoming a 2 per-center. Focus on your Pro-Vision™ and set of Pro-Values™ to help you become Drift-Free in your life.

The Achievement Goals List, the Freely Give-Up Achievement Goals List, the Benchmark Goals List, the

"What No One Else Is Doing List," and the "Seems Impossible Achievement Goals List" all change because of the paradigm shift you made to fill the "hole" in your soul with Jesus Christ.

Let's examine what typically happens to the people who choose to remain the ninety-eight per-centers of the world their whole life. They are Drifters. Typically, they live life in a clockwise manner.

Allow me to use another hub diagram, The Valley of Drifters Self-Centered Wheel of Self. People are searching to fill "hole" in their soul sometimes with food, drugs, shopping, inappropriate entertainment, inappropriate relationships, sports, and more of the good life.

I know I was in that situation many times before I gave my life to Christ. I thought I was having fun. I thought life was all about having fun, but looking back on it, it was a very destructive time in my life.

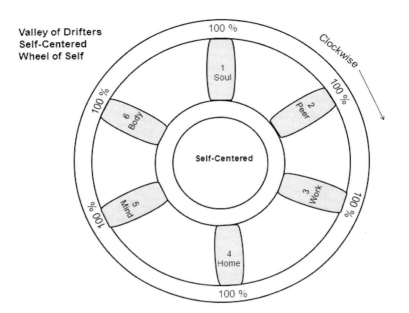

The Drifter continues to try to search for just the right "thing" to fill that "hole," Drifters search forever to find the perfect fit. They will never find it, because they are looking for it from the world's perspective – clockwise and not God's perspective – counter clockwise!

People who Drift have no Soul Goal. Spoke #1 may not even exist! If it does exist, there often appears to be no growth or the growth is superficial. This fact tends to make the whole wheel shaky and unbalanced.

Traveling in a clockwise manner, they do not find their Peer group fulfilling and Drift from one relationship to another relationship looking for the perfect fit. Love is seen as a noun, a state of being. Love is an action word. It is something you have to do. It is seen in an Eros way (sexual) not agape, which is unconditional love. Spoke #2 the Peer spoke is not very strong, either.

The Difference Between Eros Love and Agape Love

Eros love deals with sexual aspects of love. It can be very confusing to us. Why is the sexual part of love good in marriage, but not outside of marriage? Why wait? The answer is that it is a Commandment.

Agape love is unconditional love. Earlier I spoke about walking my dog, Buster. Buster demonstrates unconditional love to me on a daily basis. In fact, our Lord gave me a term for it, "being dogful'.

"Being dogful' means that no matter what happens my dog will love me. Yes, I chastise my dog when he does something wrong, but in a little while he'll come back to love me like he did before.

That's the kind of love Christ has for us. He loves us unconditionally. There are no preconceived, "I'll love you if conditions." There just is love…unconditionally.

Going in a clockwise manner to Spoke #3 work is not as fulfilling as they thought it would be. Because they keep changing their values and have no vision, they are frustrated at work. Work is seen as a means to an end. There is usually little joy in what Drifters tend to do for a living.

Typically, in Spoke #2 and Spoke #3 is where Drifters hunt for a mate. Eventually they get married. But in Spoke #4 – Home, they are not happy here, either. They continue to Drift, always looking for what's happening. They are looking for the next great adventure or they are caught in a rut.

This phenomenon can happen to Christians, too. They are looking for adventures, too. They lose their focus because they are not living through a Pro-Vision™ and a set of Pro-Values™. They try to have life both ways, as a Christian and as a non-Christian.

Let's continue on this clockwise journey. Because life eats up too much time with the first three spokes in a clockwise world, there's not much time left for other things, for example, things like taking care of your Mind. There is even less time to take care of your Body. These spokes tend to disappear from a Drifter's wheel all together.

This is what a clockwise Drifter's life looks like. Drifters drift through each day that they are on God's earth. It's not pretty.

The choice is yours. Would you rather continue to be a majority as a Drifter, one of the ninety-eight per-centers on the earth? Or would you like to become a Drift-Free person and be a two per-center?

Level 8

Rolf recently introduced me to Level 8 – Beyond Impossible. To me, Beyond Impossible is where God fits right in.

If Level 7 is Seems Impossible, the Level 8 is definitely Beyond Impossible. From a Christian perspective God operates or functions or leads at <u>all</u> 7 Levels, but Beyond Impossible is His special realm.

This is the Level that cannot be explained in human terms. Oh, we try to explain rationally as to the why or how something happens or happened, but it is inadequate because we are inadequate. We did not create the earth or ourselves.

For example, scientists have been trying to explain how the earth was formed. Some scientists have come up with the Big Bang theory. No one can prove it. It is a rational theory.

From a Christian perspective that explanation is totally inadequate. Just turn to the first chapter of Genesis and the beginning of the earth is all laid out.

This explanation doesn't work for those who believe that man came first and then the invention of religion or god.

That reminds me of the discovery by Galileo (1564-1642) that the earth rotates around the sun.

The church believed in Galileo's day that the earth was the center of the universe. The sun revolved around the earth.

The church forced Galileo to recant his findings.
It was later proven that Galileo was right. The church was wrong.

This is the Level 8 in action – Beyond Impossible.

In 2011, I flew to Huntsville, AL, to visit my two middle brothers. I took the youngest, Frank, to visit the U.S. Space Center. It is a huge complex. It's hard to imagine traveling into outer space, yet, it has been done. Just like the walls of Jericho of old seemed impossible to penetrate, so did the "walls" of space seem impossible to explore. Yet, we've even landed on the moon and returned!

Is there more to do? Of course, yes there is. The point I am making is that the vision needs to be defined before the climbers will make the climb.

Let me close with a quote from Leonardo de Vinci (1452-1519) that I saw displayed at the Space Center. "When once you have tasted flight, you will forever walk the earth with your eyes turned skyward, for there you have been and there you will long to return."

This reminds me of what mountain climbing is like. Once you have experienced climbing the summit, you will always be looking skyward.

Level 8 Level Fear: Beyond Impossible.

Level 8 is the Level of Fear of Beyond Impossible. This is where we doubt God can provide.

We overcome this fear by having 100% faith in our Lord and His ways. Be a Drift-Free climber for life along the Mountain of **BLƎ IƎ FS!®**. Make a difference along the way!

About the Authors

Coach Ed Cerny 148 Citadel Dr., Conway, SC 29526
843.347.5149 winners@sccoast.net www.coached.com

Dr. Ed Cerny (pronounced Sir-knee – means "black" in Czech) grew up all over the world as an Army brat – Europe, the Pacific Rim, the Caribbean and the U.S. He has successfully coached at both the high school and college ranks. His business experience includes being a textile marketing executive for the Allied Chemical Corp. in NYC and a marketing and sales director for several Nautilus Fitness Centers.

Ed earned a BA from the University of Kentucky, an MBA from Fordham University in NYC and a Ph.D. from USC. Dr. Cerny was a business professor at Coastal Carolina University from 1983 to 1995.

He is the author of <u>Notes From the Coach</u>, <u>Learn to Market Yourself</u>, <u>Old Coaches Never Die, We Just Run Out Of Timeouts!</u> The books are on Amazon.com.

In 1995 Dr. Cerny founded the Coach's Corner. Ed is known as "The Encouragement Coach." He works with both companies & individuals to help others reach their potential.

Ed and his wife, Zoë Ann, have been married since 1971. Zoë Ann is a faculty member at our local community college. The Lord has blessed them with four great children, and five wonderful grandchildren. The family has been active in the Fellowship of Christian Athletes since 1976.

Colonel Rolf C. Smith, Jr., USAF (Retired) 907 Alamo Road, Fredericksburg, TX 78624 830.992.2122 Basecamp@thinking-expedition.com www.thinking-expedition.com

Rolf Smith spent 24 creatively controversial years with the U.S. Air Force including 10 years in Germany and NATO in Command Control Communications Computers & Intelligence (C^4I). In 1986 he created the first military Office of Innovation and a worldwide network of military Innovation Centers. His decorations include the Defense Superior Service Medal, Legion of Merit, Bronze Star Medal, and the Air Force Meritorious Service Medal. A champion competitive shooter with the M-1 rifle at long range, he holds the Distinguished Rifleman Badge in Gold.

When he retired from active duty, he launched the Office of Strategic Innovation, Inc., and in 1988 founded the School for Innovators. From 1987-1992 he was a contract executive with Exxon, spearheading Marketing's Innovation Initiative. His passion lies in leading corporate Thinking Expeditions to explore difficult problems and unusual opportunities – and he has led Thinking Expeditions for organizations such as ExxonMobil, Texaco, IBM, Johnson & Johnson, Procter & Gamble, General Mills, EDS, Avery Dennison, CSC, DuPont, Ford, the Army, Navy, NASA, and Houston Independent School District.

An explorer, Rolf enjoys anything challenging, complex and different. In 1983 he journeyed 2,000 kilometers across Zaire with the Camel Trophy, has hunted in Zimbabwe, Tanzania, Namibia, South Africa, Kenya, Europe and Argentina. His interests change constantly but always involve experiment, discovery, learning, thinking diffferent - and mistakes.

In 1997 he authored The 7 Levels of Change (3rd Edition 2011), a field guide for thinking diffferent - adopted in 2008 as a textbook by Disney University. He has served on the board of the American Creativity Association (ACA) and the Creative Education Foundation (CEF).

Rolf graduated from the University of San Diego with a B.A. in Mathematics & Journalism and holds graduate degrees in Computer Science from Texas A&M University with extensive post-graduate PhD work in Artificial Intelligence – developing one of the first computer chess programs to play competitively. He and his wife Juliane live on their ranch near Fredericksburg in the Texas Hill Country with an eclectic collection of parrots, dogs, cats, Longhorns, llamas, horses, and various other animals. Their six children all escaped successfully but visit them frequently.

Juliane Smith, 907 Alamo Road, Fredericksburg, TX 78624   830.992.2122
juliane@mousescapes.net

I am a Christian woman, married to a loving man, who allows me to be me. Mom, Homemaker, Wife.
Teacher in the United States, Germany and Austria.

Artist and owner of the Hill County Miniatures Museum, a gallery of dollhouse size miniature works of art.

Rock Climbing Instructor, Art Instructor
Rancherette at Heart and Star Ranch, Fredericksburg, Texas

Animal Rescuer – birds, llamas, horses, cats, dogs, sheep, goats.

Author of instructional articles and writing coach to Dr. Cerny.

INFP – introverted, intuitive, feeler, perceiver, who responds to the word "help!".

Life verse: "Create in me a clean heart, O God, and renew a right spirit within me." Psalm 51:10

Pro-Vision™: Love God, Love others, Forgive.

Pro-Values™: **H**ave a heart for God's Children
Express gratitude for God's goodness
Love God, Love Others
Praise God for His grace
Enjoy God's creatures and creation
Remove my sins by your power and mercy, God, teach me, heal me, comfort me.

Appreciation

In this adventure I believe that Jesus Christ is the true lead--guide and we are all roped in together as we climb this virtual Mountain of **BƎ LIƎ FS!**® together. I am the servant at the end of the rope.

This is the first time I have tried to write a book in this manner. I have a number of co-authors to thank for their involvement, creativity, and contribution to this endeavor.

I would like to humbly thank all those who contributed to the making of this book:

Mary Boulanger	Don Green	John Rickenbacker
Simon Brand	Steve Hammond	Joni Rickenbacker
Denise Brand	Howard Henry	Danny Robinson
Zac Burkett	Michelle Henry	Lisa Robinson
Gail Byrd	Bryan Howard	Jill Rohler
Morgan Byrd	Ken Hucks	Billy Russell
Ronny Byrd	Laura Hucks	Durwin Sharp
Frank Cerny	Germaine Huxhold	Greg Shirley
Jeff Cerny	Mark Huxhold	Greg Sisson
Jim Cerny	Fabienne Jacquet	Bill Solomon
Zach Cerny	Derek McDowell	Andrea Steadman
Zoe Ann Cerny	Lindsay McDowell	James Steadman
Jon Cordas	Barbara McKewin	Diana Thompson
John Davidson	Jeff McKinney	Will Thompson
Farrah Dickerson	Sue McKinney	John Tolson
Steve Farmer	Phil Newsome	Kelly Touchstone
Bitsy Farmer	Susan Newsome	Steve Warren
Tricia Garwood	Keith Powell	Trish Warren
Paul Germeraad	Renee Powell	Anastasia Wenz
Joan Goff	Suzanne Renfrow	Pat Williams
Myranda Goff	Tim Renfrow	Mark Wolfe
Dianne Green		Debbie Wolfe

Bibliography

Collins, Jim, and Porras, Jerry, *Built to Last: Successful Habits of Visionary Companies* (New York: HarperCollins Publishers, 2001)

Collins, Jim, *Good to Great: Why Some Companies Make the Leap...and Others Don't* (New York: HarperCollins Publishers, 2001)

Collins, Jim, and Hansen, Morton, *Great by Choice: Uncertainly, Chaos, and Luck – Why Some Thrive Despite Them All* (New York: HarperCollins Publishers, 2011)

Hill, Napoleon, *Outwitting the Devil: The Secret to Freedom and Success* Annotated by Sharon Lechter with The Napoleon Hill Foundation (New York: Sterling Publishing Co., Inc., 2011)

Maltz, Maxwell, *Psycho-Cybernetics: A New Technique for Using Your SUBSCIOUS POWER* (N. Hollywood, CA: Wilshire Book Company, 1978)

Smith, Rolf, *The 7 Levels of Change: Diffferent Thinking for Different Results* (Reading PA, Tapestry Press, First Edition, 1997)

Tolson, John, *Take a Knee: Winning Plays for the Game of Life* (High Impact Life Ministries, 2011)

Williams, Pat, with Denney, Jim, *Coach Wooden: The 7 Principles That Shaped His Life and Will Change Yours* (Grand Rapids, MI: Published by Revell, 2011)

Wooden, John, *They Call Me Coach* (Waco, TX: Word Books, Publisher, 1972)